Psychosomatic
Act 1 Scene 1 Episode 1

The female voice speaks: "the movie set scene
is the largest auditorium in New York, you see all
the people it takes to make a typical movie scene,
the producer, directors, the actors and actress, all
the camera crew, all of the behind the scenes
crew making this into a believable scene, the
camera zooms in on a man with a baseball hat
and sunglasses with a remote control joy stick in
his hand, you see the drone helicopter take off
with a camera attached, you now can see an
aerial view of everything, yes a birds eye view as
you hear the producers voice say "Quiet on the
set, let's roll em, action" again as you see various
film scenes the female voice speaks again " you
now can see the large auditorium, yes the largest
auditorium in New York, as hundreds of cars are
pulling in, people getting out and going in the
front door, the drone backs off and shows a
beautiful black cherry 1949 Rolls Royce going
around the side to the back entrance, the sky is
blue, it's a beautiful spring day as the limo stops
in back, the driver door opens and you see the
bodyguard, an old cowboy with a white cowboy
hat get out, you notice his cowboy boots, blue
jeans and you notice his bullet proof vest under
his cowboy shirt, you notice the star badge and
the two six shooters with pearl handles, you think
of Roy Rogers or hop a long Cassidy as you
smile, you notice he looks a lot like a younger
version of Sam Elliott and you wonder if it really
is, he has sunglasses on and an ear and mouth
phone, as he looks around and scans the area he
says "Looks ok" the camera zooms in on the
other side of the limo as the front passenger door
opens and out comes a beautiful oriental woman,
wearing a bullet proof vest she is wearing a
shoulder harness with a Glock 9mm, black pants,
black boots, you realize she is a female version of
Bruce Lee, Yes, she was trained well, she too is
wearing sunglass and ear and mouth phone as

she scan the area, she too says "Looks ok she opens her back door and an elegant older lady comes out as the other side, he opens his back door and the olde man with a black cowboy hat gets out, you notice he has a long handlebar moustache too, he is wearing a cowboy shirt, blue jeans and lizard cowboy boots, in one hand he is carrying a Holy Bible, the two body guards escort the olde man inside, they are greeted by several people and do the normal hand shaking and greetings they are all escorted to the stage area were they are all seated, now we wait for all the people to get in, settle down and get started, the male Body guard is Rex Rogers, he was a Texas Ranger in his younger days, he takes his sunglasses off as he looks at his watch and says, "We got about ten minutes, ok"? The female body Guard is Jasmine Lee, his wife, she nods her head in agreement as she too takes her sunglasses off scans the area and sets on one side of the woman, she is the wife, the camera zooms out to the audience as you see hundreds of people walk in the front entrance, as people escort them down the aisle and they talk among themselves you notice the drone helicopter with the camera is now inside the Hugh auditorium and you see the guy take his sunglasses off as he flies the drone around showing a cool aerial view inside the massive auditorium showing the second floor balcony with hundreds of people going in upstairs too, all want to see the famous one dog and one pony show get started, they all read all the crazy, fictional books/screenplays he has wrote over the last 20 plus years, and heard the crazy Olde man, the Rebellious teacher, a pile of books and a holy bible in one hand and a bottle of whiskey in the other hand, fighting demons, the religious system and the educational system trying to teach to a world that does not want to know the truth, talking about this world being forsaken, we have twisted religions around so much, we are scattered, divided and confused to say the least and Lucifer is laughing his ass off at how stupid and gullible you pathetic mortal,

temporary, flesh and blood temporary humans
are to manipulate. The sad part is there are over
2 billion so called Christians who claim that and
90% are wrong walking around like zombie's
without a clue, yes this world teaches
Psychosomatic, it is all in your mind, it is hard to
imagine over 2 billion so called Christians out
there who have been lied to mis lead and not
even wanting to know the truth You notice a lot of
the behind the scenes activity showing all the
different camera showing a different angle with all
the extra people it takes to make a typical movie
set, then a man walks up to the podium and
introduces himself and thanks all the people for
coming here, as the audience quiets down he
introduces the old man as the Rebellious
Teacher, trying to change religion and telling
everyone that all Religions are a scam is crazy,
they all want to hear his side of his story, as the
audience all mumbles their likes and dislikes, the
olde man, smiles, holds one hand up to quiet the
audience and stands before the microphone and
you can also read his words: "Thank you for
inviting me here to your auditorium, a lot of
people have read some of my books/
screenplays, I wrote over a hundred at
Amazon.com and won 40 international fil festival
awards from all over the world so far, thank you
Film freeway," He stops, the female voice speaks
"he smiles, as the camera films, you notice the
puff of black smoke enter his mouth and his eyes
turn glossy black, you know the demonic entity is
inside of the olde man, he reaches in his back
pocket for his bottle of whiskey and you notice his
hand shape shift into this demonic hand with
long, scary fingernails as he pulls the bottle out,
smiling, you notice his other hand shape shifts
into the demonic scary hand with long fingernails
as he opens the bottle of whiskey, takes a drink,
licks his lips, screws the cap back on and puts the
bottle of whiskey back into his back pocket then
everything goes back to normal, you see his eyes
and everything is normal as he speaks: "the
greatest trick Lucifer ever played on mankind was

convincing them he was their God so they would follow him no matter what else they may see and hear. if you do not remember anything else remember that, I realize the things I am saying will piss a lot of so called Christians off, it is not only the 2 plus billion, Christians but all religions, Islam, Jewish, Hindu and buddha, what right do I have to say I am right and the whole world is wrong? I know if I was wrong, or if someone was at least telling me I am wrong, I would want to know the truth, If someone told me all the things I was taught from the day I was born, I would at Least give them the courtesy to listen to them and then make my decision, no one wants to give me that courtesy, no one wants to at least hear what I am saying, the demons and the demonic entities out there do not want you to hear this so they are telling you to not listen and there is nothing I can do about that. My books/screenplays continue where the book, the Movie the Da Vinci code left off back in 2004, great book by Dan Brown and a great movie by producer Ron Howard who gave him 6 million to make his one book into a movie, starring Tom Hanks, who was a imaginary Harvard Symbologist who said God, Yahweh has a wife, Shekhinah, queen of heaven, the Holy spirit, the Holy Ghost, the Holy grail and Jesus was married to Mary Magdalene, a Jewish Hebrew woman from the tribe of Benjamin and they had lots of kids and his bloodline is still out there today, we now realize Jesus Christ is a Jewish Hebrew Rabbi who kept the Torah, the Tanakh, the Law, Jesus never worshipped on Sunday, the 1st day of the week, as a Jewish Hebrew Rabbi he kept the 7th day Saturday sabbath as they still do today, His mother, the virgin Mary was from the Hebrew tribe of Levi and his earthly father, Joseph was from the right tribe of Judah, the lion of Judah, to bring forth the Messiah, the Ha Mashiach to be the Ha Mashiach but the Jewish people would not accept him, Why? Did they find out Jesus was never butchered, never circumcised? Remember all we know is the story in the holy bible, Joseph and

Mary were in Bethlehem to pay their share of taxes, the baby was born, Jewish custom is to wait 7 days and butcher the baby boy by cutting the foreskin off the fore head of the penis by changing what God created and putting a permanent mark on the forehead of the baby boy, we know a angel told joseph and Mary to flee to Egypt because king Herod wanted to kill the baby, did they wait the customary 8 days, butcher the son of God or did God say do not change my son? What right do we have to change what God created? If we look at the history and read the bible. Lucifer told God he could change his chosen people by putting a permanent mark on all the male Hebrew, And God did not think his chosen people would fall for that lie, so God allowed Lucifer to convince the Hebrew people to get a butcher knife and cut the foreskin off their forehead of all males because it was a clean issue, they were in the desert and a lack of water, but now 2,000 years later Lucifer is still convincing the chosen Hebrew who are now called the Jewish name and still butchering innocent babies, calling it a tradition of circumcision, but what gives anyone the right to change what God created? Did God butcher Adam or any of his male sons, grandsons? No Did Noah butcher any of his sons, grandsons etc? No then why do we say we are in a desert and too lazy to wash so we will put a permanent mark on a innocent baby by getting a butcher knife and cutting the foreskin off marking that baby with the mark of the beast to show they do not obey God, later the islam were also living in the desert and they followed that butchering tradition even now with plenty of water still butchering innocent baby boys at the 8th day of birth, why? Again what gives us the right to change what God created? Are we too lazy to pull the foreskin back and wash it or will we still let Lucifer and all his demons still put a permanent mark of the beast on their forehead, but you say that is different that is a foreskin on the head and not the forehead, we know the original words were written on whatever they could find stone or a animal skin and thru the years has to be updated and added and moved to suit the powers in charge, we now created a free ministry that openly talks about all this it is now a knights of Avalon church ministry, a non-denominational open church, no matter what color skin, hair or eyes, no matter what previous religion you were taught or believe in, does it have to be just a Christian Church only? Can we use the same never pass an offering plate around by having a box by the entrance saying Tithes, offerings and prayer request? As a Christian we were taught we have this illusion we only get one life, and we all get to spend an eternity in heaven forever and ever, will there only be Christians up in your version of heaven? What about all the other religions? What about all the millions. billions of people born and created before our Jesus was born? We see all these versions of a non-denominational type cowboy church and now a fishermen type church, as a non-denominational Christian Church only, can an Islam, a Buddha, a Hindu or a Jewish person ride a horse or be a cowboy, or actually go fishing? We do know Jesus did ride on a donkey, we know they had cows and bulls back then, we know the Jewish people would sacrifice a young calf or bull for religion purposes, you commit a sin. get a calf or a lamb to sacrifice for your sins, they did do away with this animal sacrificial law, why should an innocent calf or bull die for your sins anyway? Would the world be a little bit better place if we call this A Brotherhood type church and invite all different religions to come and fellowship with us? Could we have an Immortality Cowboy church, an Knights of Avalon Fishermen church, and a Brotherhood type church in the same town. Maybe even down the street from each other like the different Baptist, Methodist, Catholic and other denominations do some even across the street from each other? Can we gain anything by joining together, as brothers and sisters, and share our love for our creator no matter what name we want to call them? Is God, Yahweh the same God as Jehovah, Allah, Buddha, Odin, Jupiter, Osiris, Cerrunos, or Zeus? Can we all share some of the different names we all call our female side of God, the Hebrew Goddess, Shekhinah, is that the same as Juno, Hera, Isis, Freya or Cerridwen? In my younger days I rode a Motorcycle, I was part of the Biker Brotherhood, we stood together as brothers and sisters, helping each other out all for one and one for all, we had a secret handshake that only members of the brotherhood knew, instead of just shaking your hand, we look each other in the eye, reach our hand out and put our hand on their forearm, behind the hand, grab their forearm and shake, then pull each other closer, and pat each other on the back as true Brothers and sisters, some add the closed fist touching the others closed fist and then say boom as our fist opens up showing a mental explosion, this was our secret handshake, only a member of the Brotherhood can share with someone they know or want to be a part of the Brother hood, you see someone who is mean, hateful or you do not want them to be a part of YOUR Brotherhood, then you do not look them in the eye, you do not reach out and give them the secret handshake with the closed fist explosion, only a true pure brother or sister understands the real Power of the real Brotherhood, we stand by each other, better or worse, we help each other out, one has a problem, we all have a problem, we are true, pure Brothers and sisters, yes our sisters are Equal, you would not be here if a sister or mother created you. In every one of my books/screenplays, I share a lot of the same stories, why? If you are in school and you know there is going to be a test, then you study over and over the things that are important, that might be on a test, this is school, I get to be the teacher, this time around and we are in the class called life 101 I am an Immortal spirit soul and so are you, I have lived many lifetimes and so have you, Jesus taught Re-Incarnation" He stops hold his Holy Bible up in the air, showing everyone his version and says: " This is the Liberty University, Jerry Falwell, Faith Partners edition, I grew up as a typical good old Baptist, a lot of my family are still good old Baptist, all you know is what you were taught, all they can teach you is what they were taught, it's obvious someone was taught wrong about a giant circular staircase, why? It's such a great story that bears repeating over and over, as a prodigal son myself, I had the wild rebellion attitude, letting the devil show me the wild side of life, as you look up and down this circular staircase do you see some of your Brotherhood, maybe lower or up higher? For those who never heard the story, we can imagine everyone in the world on a giant, circular staircase, millions, billions, trillions of people, all on this giant circular staircase, it does not matter what step you are on at this moment, but you are on a certain step, you can look up and see thousands, millions of people on a higher step, you are not mad or jealous, you understand maybe they are older then you, maybe they know things you do not know, you can also look down and see millions of people on a lower step then you, then you realize maybe this is why your creator, does not matter whether you see a male God, a female Goddess, both, neither or whatever you see now maybe this is why you have two arms, maybe if you raise one arm up in the air, maybe someone, who is on a higher step, maybe they will reach down, show you what you need to know to climb up that one step, just maybe, then with the other hand you are now looking down, you understand, you were down there too, yes you are the prodigal run away son, you been thru hell and high water, there were people who walked by, ignoring you but then there were those, maybe a brotherhood or not, who did reach out with a helping hand to pull you up a step, that is what this book/ screenplay is all about, I wish I could give all of this to you for free, I have to go thru Amazon.com, they have to convert my crazy ideology into a book, they buy the paper, ink and pay someone to push the buttons to make all this

into a book/screenplay, yes, they call me a
Rebellious Teacher, this is all about the
Brotherhood, a Holy Bible in one hand and a
bottle of whiskey in the other, yes, fighting
Demons and preaching to a world that does not
want to know the truth. Who created the Devil?"
He pauses, looks around at the massive
audience, takes a drink of whiskey, again did you
notice the puff of black smoke going into his
eyes? Did you notice his eyes turn glossy black
for a second? Did you notice his hands shapeshift
into a monster scary hand with long fingernails for
a second? then continues, "If our God, Yahweh
and our Goddess, Shekinah created everything
then did they create Satan? Why? How do you
know if something is good or evil unless someone
teaches you? What better teacher then Lucifer,
the first-born son, created long before our Jesus
Christ, long before Adam, Eve and this world was
created. Was Lucifer the real first-born son? The
only one who has the right to one day rule over
something? Is this why Lucifer and a third of his
Brothers and sisters were in a rebellion? So, is
Lucifer and Jesus blood brothers? Same Father
and same Mother? Oh, I forgot you do not believe
in a female Goddess. all you know is what you
were taught, all they can teach you is what they
were taught, what if you were taught wrong,
would you want to know the Truth? Can you
handle the truth? Someone is right, someone is
wrong, who gets to decide, you are right, and you
are wrong? What is right for one person is wrong
for another. we are all here to experience the
things we need to experience during this lifetime.
Half of the world does believe in Re-incarnation.
The fastest growing religion today is Wicca, the
sacred feminine, the Holy Ghost, the Holy Grail,
the Shekinah, Queen of Heaven, the part of the
Da Vinci code, now the rest of the story." He
stops, looks down at his Jack Daniel whiskey
bottle and says, "This is a bottle of whiskey, it
helps shut up the demons inside of me, trying to
control what I say. In one of my past lives, I was
there when they nailed our Jesus Christ on the

cross. I was nobody special, just one of a thousand, watching and knowing any minute, God would bring a thousand angels and show the world that our Jesus Christ is the Son of our God, but no, we all cried out and asked why?? I realized I was an immortal spirit soul. I have lived many lifetimes and so have you. Each life, my immortal spirit soul goes into a new, flesh and blood, temporary, mortal body to experience the things I need to experience during each lifetime. Each life I keep the same fingerprint to identify me from billions of others. The debate was a good one, some understand maybe a brotherhood is a good thing, we all are really brothers and sisters, we all call our God Father, then we all are sons and daughters, we can imagine all the other preachers explaining why it's ok to worship a male dominant God on Sunday the 1st day of the week, instead of keeping the ten commandments and the original 7th day Saturday sabbath and why they think we are all saved by grace and yes we get to live in heaven forever and ever or burn in a fiery hell forever and ever, they just admitted they too are an immortal spirit soul so now they understand the book/screenplay Immortality does make sense. It is time to teach the secrets of Yeshua. When you realize everything in creation came from a female, every human, animal, bird and fish did come from a female and when your mortal temporary flesh and blood, human, animal, bird and fish body dies, it too will go back to a female, we call her Mother Earth or Mother Nature. Actually that is her daughter, Auriel, her spirit will enter the old man's body and use him to explain these things, Now you understand why most Christians do not worship the female in this creation process, they want to call the female a witch or a vampire, they assume we all drink blood and worship the devil, yes I created Lucifer, the first born son, how do you know if something is good or evil unless someone teaches you? What better teacher then the first-born Son (sun)? Yes, I am the Goddess, Shekinah, wife of your God, Yahweh." Now next

act the next scene, the sky is blue the camera shows the drone airplane, which also has a camera hook up so you can see a bird's eye view of everything, the camera scans the beautiful ocean front mansion below. The bodyguard's booth at the massive front gate, the massive swimming pool with a waterfall overlooking the ocean, you hear the seagulls and hear the ocean waves. The voice is an old man with years of wisdom slowly laughing and talking ."I am a vampire, I like to think, thru the years, and many lifetime's I became civilized, so in my mind, I tell everyone that I do not drink blood or turn into a bat, that is all Hollywood hype, a real Vampyre drinks your power, your energy, your orgasm, leaving you drained and smiling, wanting more. I have lived many lifetimes and so have you" as the drone shows different angles as the front door opens and you see the butler and the plane dives in as the butler ducks out of the way. Another camera crew is showing the old man walking up to the big mansion with the control stick in his hand laughing like a ten-year-old as he runs by the butler to see where his toy plane went to. The camera crew follows filming different angels, and another camera crew is filming the behind-the-scenes part showing what the other camera crew are doing. You see all the people it takes to make a scene, yes this is just another act another scene, you now see the drone airplane flying around the massive entry with the beautiful crystal chandelier and the big, massive, curved staircase. The film crew follows, you see one of the cooks as the old man enters, she says " are you hungry?" "Yes" says the olde man as he sets at the beautiful oak table large enough for twenty people to set at, The camera crew shows different scenes thru out the massive house and the second camera crew shows all the behind the scenes of the first camera crew, each angle and now you get to see not only the movie scene but all the little things it takes to create a movie set .
End of chapter 1 act1 scene 1
The Invisible Umbilical cord by Melvin

Abercrombie
From concievement, till the day you were born
A Umbilical cord was there, Not to be torn,
until the day you arrive and start to cry,
and everyone amazed ask the reason why
How can our God create, from nothing it seems,
Now 9 months later, you are holding the dream.
Although the umbilical cord has long been gone,
An invisible one replaces it, for your never alone,
For everyone involved, including God above,
sends out these feelings, the emotions of love,
on invisible cords from you to me,
if we had special glasses, then we could see,
a thousand and thousand cords going away,
like a bowl of spaghetti, what would you say,
everyone has them from all that they love,
family ,friends, neighbors and those up above,
loved ones that died, are not really gone,
for the cord is still there, you are never alone,
So wisdom, knowledge and understanding too,
is sent thru this cord from me to you.
Copyright 2006   www.poetry.com   by Melvin

Abercrombie   **Chapter**

2 act 2 scene 2

Next act, Next scene is your typical lecture
seminar in another city, another state about the
book screenplay Psycho somatic, you can add
special effect scenes as needed, the olde man
getting a drink of whiskey as his eyes turn glossy
black showing the demon is again inside him and
showing his hands and maybe other parts of his
body shape shift for a second as he gets ready to
speak " Thank you for allowing me here, those
who already read some of my books/screenplays
know I do a lot of over and over topics, again, I
apologize but that is how I remember things, I
love the United states of America and I thank my
God, my Goddess and My Jesus for letting me be
born here, I have no problem with people coming
over from other countries to better themselves,
we all have ancestors who migrated from different
countries to be here, We have slowly evolved into

the land of the free, illegals can come over here,
not even bother to speak our English language,
demand we give them free welfare, free food
stamps and free section 8 housing, you want to
stop this, then you have to stop giving away free,
again I do not blame them for wanting free stuff,
we spend millions, billions on trying to build a wall
to keep these illegals out. Imagine you are the
president, governor or leader of a large city in a
different country, you have a jail system there
where you have to lock up, feed and take care of
murderers, drug addicts, crime lords gang
members, they all have normal families, wives,
husbands children who now do not get the money
they were getting because now they are locked
up in a jail system for the next 20 plus years, How
do you get rid of that problem, it is costing your
government a lot of money to take care of, feed
and hire guards to watch over them, solution?
You get them and their families, change their
identification papers, put them on a one way bus
to America and do not ever come back, the
government takes all your possessions, house
land etc and you have no place to go but to
America where you get free section 8 housing,
free food stamps and free welfare a chance to
change and live a better life, do you take it? What
choice do you have? Now you are in America, do
you get a American Driver license? How do you
get from your free section 8 housing to the free
grocery store? You have any money? Is our
government going to pay for your down payment
on a car? What about the monthly payments, who
pays that every month? What about Insurance for
this car to get you back and forth, maybe try to
find a job? Who buys the gasoline to put into this
automobile? You have very few clothes so who
buys your shoes, socks, underwear, panties,
pants shirts, dress, blouse for you your wife and
all your kids? Sure eventually you will get a job,
learn our English language, and then pay your
share of taxes or get another fake id card and
move to another city, another state and do it over
and over again because no one checks your

fingerprint, the last place you were at destroyed
all copies of your fingerprint file and make you
think these people are all good Christian people
wanting to better themselves, Yes, most are
could there be a few drug lords or gang members
mixed in to get rid of them? Instead of spending
billions and billions on trying to build a wall to
keep these illegals out help these countries
create their own welfare system in their own
countries then these people do not have to leave
their families, we could build Quality apartment
section 8 housing right there in their own
countries giving local people a job clean up their
country why is the United states of America the
only country in the world offering free welfare,
free food stamps, free section 8 housing, stop the
free, they stop coming or help build this in their
country, we spend billions and billions of aide
who gets all this? A very few greedy power
people very little trickles down to the real needy, it
is all Psychosomatic it is all in your mind or is it?
End of chapter 2

Yahshua, My Savior

I was there when they nailed him to a cross,
A nameless person, in a crowd of the lost,
A thousand or more people all wanting to see,
the son of our God, what would he be?
would a legion of Angels, come out of the blue,
to take him away, if his words are all true,
but no, we cried and to our dismay,
He hung and died on that cross that day,
so stubborn and stupid, not wanting to believe,
the reality of our God, so simple to conceive,
He had to die for all of mankind,
so the sacrificial law, we would no longer find,
How can I live now, and live back then,
is it only a dream, or remembering when,
all the little things of life, every day,
the feelings, the hurt but what do you say,
if you truly believe, that one day you die,
then in another life wake up and wonder why,
I was there when they nailed him to a cross,
A nameless person in a crowd of the lost.
Copyright 2006 www.poetry.com by Melvin

Abercrombie

act 3 scene 3 episode 3

The scene is another lecture seminar, another city another state, you can add special effects and shape shifting scenes at will, He stands before the microphone and says, " Hello everyone this is about my book screenplay Psychosomatic, is it all in your mind? When you dream, you leave your physical flesh and blood human, mortal body and do a out of body experience was all this Psychosomatic? Where you really there in that other dimension, did you touch things in that other world? Did you leave your fingerprint there? Can only flesh and blood humans have a fingerprint? We do know some monkeys and apes do have a fingerprint. A day will come we will add to our computer system everyone who is born, when they die we will figure out to put that fingerprint in a archive file and see if we actually come back in another lifeform and keep the same fingerprint over and over? You are so special no one has your fingerprint, millions and billions of people out there and no one has your fingerprint, but under your psychosomatic world you live in you were taught you only get to live one lifetime, this is what you were taught, must be true, millions and billions of false Christians have been lied to for almost 2,000 years thinking they are right, you get one lifetime you get to go to a heaven, go thru the pearly gates and set in your mansion forever and ever, must be so, or you will burn in a fiery hell forever and ever does not matter if you killed one person or a hundred there is only one heaven and one hell, the greatest trick Lucifer ever played on mankind was convincing them he was their God so they would follow him no matter what else they may see and hear, does that sound like something Psychosomatic to you?? They call me the olde man, a rebellious teacher, a pile of books and a holy bible in one hand and a bottle of whiskey in the other hand, fighting demons, the religious system and the educational system, trying to teach to a world that does not want to know the truth, I am an immortal spirit soul, and so are you, I have lived many lifetimes and so have you, yes in one of my past life I was there when the Romans nailed our Jesus Christ on the cross, I was nobody special, just one of a thousand watching and knowing any minute, our God would bring down a thousand Angels, then the world would know he is the true Son of our God, Yahweh, but no, to our dismay, God allowed Him to die that day, I did not understand why then, but now I understand Jesus had to die to do away with the animal sacrificial law, Why should a innocent animal die for something you did anyway? I am the author of over a hundred books at Amazon, Trafford publishing, Barnes and Noble, Books a million and Ebay," As he looks out at the vast audience Brigitte setting on the front row, as he looks at her, she smiles and uncrosses her legs so he can see, she does not have any panties on, the old man flushed and turned his head as he continued " I remember as a kid 60 years ago reading about King Arthur and the knights of the round table, yes they were all on a quest to find the holy grail, only when he was on his deathbed did the females allow him to go thru the vail, the fog, and get on the boat and see the healing island of Avalon. If you read the book and saw the movie, the Da Vinci Code, then you realize they found part of the Holy Grail, God does have a wife, she is shekinah, queen of heaven and Jesus was married to Mary Magdalene and had children, they believed the bloodline of Jesus was still alive, that's what the book and movie was all about, but now what happened? Where is the church now? where is the religion that offers equality? What happened to the Brotherhood? What happens next? We always thought there must be a female somewhere in this creation process and the religion, wicca and Da Vinci code proves that what about the rest of the story? My books continue were the Da Vinci code left off. I found the other keys that opened the rest of the secret doors, guarded by angels and demons and found the rest of the holy grail and I found the secret keys to the brotherhood and their secret handshake as a motorcycle biker we use and did not know the power of the handshake and the power of this Brotherhood, this knowledge about immortality. If you read the book and saw the movie, the da Vinci code you realize they found one of the secret doors, why would a book and movie, sell 50 million copies and get everyone excited and talked about the goddess and the real Jesus then just stop? Sure, dan brown made millions of dollars, so they were happy, but do you want to know what else? Did Jesus teach the Brotherhood? Was His disciples a part of the Brotherhood? Did they allow woman to join this original brotherhood? Yes, of course, where is the church Jesus would go to? We know Jesus never worshipped on Sunday, the 1st day of the week, he kept the 7th day Saturday sabbath and we know Jesus never ate pork, catfish or other scavenger foods. He kept the kosher Levitical food law. We are in this age of Aquarius, the returning of the female, yes, the Goddess has always been here, we chose not to accept her and wicca was hidden from us. Now sometimes we need not just a physical healing but a mental and spiritual healing also. so, the vail is open to all who seek, the fog is removed to all who will believe, and the healing Island of Avalon is not just a physical healing place but a mental and a spiritual healing place you can go to anytime 24 hours a day, 7 days a week and 365 days of the year, all who believe and seek. I have had this reoccurring dream over and over and for a long time did not make sense, now, finally it does. the dream was a lot of doors, all locked with different type locks, some with a hasp type, others a deadbolt or regular house lock, some had to have a combination and one your fingerprint to open it, one was voice activated and I tried all the magical words I could think of and tried all my number combination and keys but could not open the doors. I finally figured there were eight doors and little at a time I found the key to open each one and wrote a different book trying to share my newfound knowledge. Only when I found the key to the last door and put all these together then I realized the holy grail is more than just what the Da Vinci code found out, yes I am glad Dan Brown wrote the book, The movie studio paid Dan Brown 6 million for the option to make his book into a movie and over 50 million dollar book sales and I am glad they made a great movie with Ron Howard as the producer and Tom Hanks' as the Harvard symbologist, now what? Where is the rest of the story? What happens next? What happened to this brotherhood, is this something only a bunch of motorcycle bikers can find out and say, yes they are a part of their Brotherhood, we help our Brothers and sisters out, all my books continue where the Da Vinci code left off, not history but Herstory, we are all looking at the world backwards. We think of ourselves as a temporary, mortal, flesh and blood human who happens to be here during this lifetime to experience the things we need to experience, when you look at the big picture and realize there are over hundred different languages, different cultures, different customs and different religions, so will all of them be up there in heaven? All the different skin colors, different languages, different religions, millions and billions of mansions? As a Christian we were taught, we live so long, then we die and get to go to a heaven or burn in a hell forever, this is what we were taught, only 2 choices, what were these other cultures taught? Can all these be in a heaven or hell forever. In reality we are all immortal spirit/ souls who have lived many lifetimes and each lifetime we are here to experience different things, and everyone now believes we finally found the holy grail. So that is going to solve all our problems, right? Yes, the movies about Angels and Demons, the Da Vinci Code and others tell you that the holy grail was not a cup or chalice that maybe the blood of Jesus was in, that miraculous healed anyone who found it. their logic is the symbol of a man is a three-pointed symbol like a triangle or pyramid with one point aiming up to show the male anatomy or penis. the symbol of a female is the opposite and that is a three-pointed upside-down triangle showing the female anatomy or vagina, the lifeline of all creation, that part is true. This has always been a universal symbol for all cultures and civilizations, End of Chapter 3 act 3 Scene 3

Wolf

The Moon was full, the stars were bright
As I wandered aimlessly, deep in the night
searching and searching, hoping to find,
the answer to my question, a one of a kind,
I asked the tree's to answer me true,
and not give a question from out of the blue,
I wanted true love, I only wanted the best,
I searched and kept looking thru all of the rest,
then the wolf told me what I wanted to hear,
that love was around, far, but also very near,
I followed the wolf and I learned a bunch,
about loyalty, faithful and following my hunch,
the cubs, the old ones, a family affair,
the rules, the Laws, that no one would dare,
disobey, out of respect for you see,
the answer was there, inside of me,
the riddle, the parable, to my dismay,
has always been in me, now hoping to say,
the moon was full, the stars were bright,
as I wandered Happily, deep in the night.
copyright 2006 www.poetry.com by Melvin Abercrombie

scene 4 act 4 Episode 4

the old man was doing another lecture seminar, a big auditorium with thousands of people listening and standing in front of a podium, wearing his old black cowboy hat and he looks up and says, " I remember as a child a long time ago reading the books about King Arthur and the knights of the round table and their quest for the holy grail thru the male place called Anglesey and the female island of Avalon. Just like the catholic today try to separate the male from the female to avoid temptation but only makes it worse. I was never a great knight that went around slaying fire breathing dragons and rescuing damsels in distress, with my name called Melvin I was always fascinated with Merlin, one letter different. I pictured myself as a good magician, helping people understand and protect those who tried to do the right thing, just as Merlin did, so I read every book I could find on wizards and sorcery, both white magick and dark magick. I got away from the Christian Baptist teachings of my family because to me it did not make sense. I read the part where Jesus said, "You have not because you ask not, ask and you shall receive." so now I asked questions and preachers could not give me a straight answer. I studied this oriental buddha and found good teaching there. I studied the Hindu, Islam, Jewish and different Christian religions. I remember a friend of mine invited me to go to a Pentecostal holy roller revival, she warned me there would be a lot of jumping around, talking tongues and all kinds of crazy stuff, my Baptist church never did do, so I went. The preacher went crazy shouting out fire and brimstone and everyone else stood up and so did I. I looked to my left and this older woman put up her hands in the air and started jumping up and down shouting halleluiah, praise the lord and took off running down the aisle, then a man on my right did the same thing and took off running and everyone put their hands up but me. they were all shouting and hollering some gibberish, so I guess this was their tongues they were talking about, part of me wanted to take off running out the back door and not look back, but then to not be different I put my hands up in the air too so no one would think I am different and as I raised my hands, this emotion came over me, goosebumps all over me and this energy force came down thru my upraised hands I never felt before. no one prepared me for this, how do I explain what happened to me then? All I can tell you is if this is the real God, then I love it, no more silent Baptist for me I wanted to feel this holy ghost, these emotions who is this God that gives me the shakes? My mission in this lifetime was to find the true church that Jesus Christ would actually go to. I went to a lot of different denominational churches, but most want you to be quiet, no chewing gum, occasionally, say amen, pass the offering plate around and everyone looks at you and sees how much money you give the church. I understand it takes a lot of money to run a church, you want a fancy building? that takes money, people expect to get paid and utilities are not free, so I do understand the cost. I was a Baptist preacher, treasurer, deacon and elder, but I kept asking myself, would the real Jesus Christ, if he was alive today, would he actually go to this church on Sunday, the 1st day of the week and always the answer was no way". so that was the end of that lecture. The voice talks:" yes Brigitte tried to behave, she knew she had her two buddies to give her all she wanted and if not, she brought her fancy vibrator, so the crew, bill and veronica filmed everything and now go back to the mansion send in all the film to the Hollywood Gossip and enjoy a few drinks and jump in the hot tub." next act, next scene, Next day, they go to another lecture in a giant church and the old man talks some more "Everyone has heard of the new world order where these billionaires are trying to get everyone to join this new club, actually it's not a new club the new world order has been around for the last 2,000 years I will prove that is why time was changed from our old B.C. or before the common era to now, what we call A.D. or after the common era, as we now call it. sounds good, to a certain extent, people sometimes hear the word new and do not like a new change. They are happy with the way it is, don't rock the boat type people and I understand that, but I grew up as a Baptist, this is all I know, what my parents and family taught me, so when I hear a new world order, I think what about the old-world order that Adam and Eve were here to experience? If it was good enough for Adam and eve, would it be good enough for me? As a Christian, I understand the teachings of the Christ and going thru theology, I now understand what we are teaching is not what the real Jesus Christ did teach. So, to me we should go back to an olde world order, during the time our Jesus did walk around on this earth as a flesh and blood mortal and do what the real Jesus Christ did do. At first, I found five secrets that Jesus Christ did teach originally and is not taught now, then I found three more, so I wrote this book with eight secret teachings, or 8 secret doors, I had to fight off demons and angels to open up, yes some of the teachings are being used by some of the people. Ask yourself one question, if Jesus Christ was alive as a flesh and blood mortal human being, which church would he go to? The answer is none, that is a shame, that there is not a church out there today that teaches all the things Jesus tried to teach. Then what about buddha? If buddha was alive, would he go to any of the churches out there? Then we ask God what church would God go to? Would God go to a typical Jewish church today? No, God has a wife, she is the holy grail, King Arthur and the knights of the round table been looking for. No church out there is showing this equality. The Da Vinci Code tried to talk about the Goddess, Shekhinah, the Holy Spirit, the Holy Ghost, this holy grail, the bloodline of Jesus showing that he was actually married, and is still alive today so now where is the church the da Vinci code tried to find? Where is the holy grail? 50 million people bought the book that dan brown did write and the producer, Ron Howard of the Andy Griffin show made a great movie, but then what happened? Where is the church that God, the father, Yahweh would go to? Where is the church showing equality with the wife of God as the Shekinah the queen of heaven? So instead of creating this new world order, which has only been around for the last two thousand years, let's go back to the olde world order that has been around for thousands and thousands of years, from the beginning of time and see what church our God, Yahweh would go to, That the Goddess, Shekinah would go to. That the real buddha and Jesus Christ would go to. You have this crazy dream or an Illusion you only get one chance at this game called life and you die and get to go to a heaven forever and ever and there will be one God, one church, one religion, one language and one people, so now we call it a new world order. The olde world order that our God created a long time ago, taught you have one male God, one female Goddess, one people, one language, one religion and when you die, you are judged and go back into a new resurrected body to experience different things during your next lifetime. There is no eternal heaven or an eternal hell, that is how a few, in charge, can control the mass by fear. Have you ever wondered why was Jesus Christ killed in the first place? We know a angel told Joseph and Mary to flee to Egypt after the baby Jesus was born, did they have time to butcher this innocent baby by Circumcision? Did our God tell them to not change what God, the father created by cutting the fore-skin off the forehead of his penis changing and putting on a mark of the beast what gives us the right to change what our God Created? Could this be something only Lucifer created? We know originally, they were in a desert, lack of water but now plenty of water could the Jewish Rabbi later found out and maybe this is one of the reasons the Jewish rabbis wanted him dead, is to silence him. Has anyone ever wondered what Jesus did that was so bad, the Jewish rabbis wanted to silence him? They were willing to let a known murderer go free, so the romans would crucify Jesus, why? Even the roman leader, Pilate washed his hands of the matter and said he found no reason to kill him, but the Jewish rabbis would not give up, they demanded Jesus to be killed, why? Again, to silence Him, what were the Brotherhood teachings the real Jesus Christ was trying to teach? Did Jesus share the secret handshake to show the true brotherhood to separate them from everyone else? Each lecture I will some of these, so now we are talking about a different topic to keep from being boring. so, we will talk about the first teaching secret. God does have a wife, yes, you call her the holy ghost, she is Shekinah, queen of heaven the wife of God. We have equality just like when Jesus was alive, remember when Jesus was alive, the romans worshipped a male God they called Jupiter and a female Goddess known as Juno. You can go to Rome Italy today and still see the statues and remnants of this God and Goddess, they call it the olde religion. It's the same with the Greeks, they called their God Zeus, and their Goddess was known as Hera and you can go to the Greek Islands and still see the remnants, the statues of the Goddess. If you go to Egypt which Moses and joseph both went to, you can see the God Osiris and the Goddess Isis and still to this day see the temple of Isis and many other cultures many other civilizations. Remember Christianity is only two thousand years old, so what did people believe in before Jesus was born? What did people read before the New Testament was written? They had the olde testament. the olde time period we call B.C. If you watch the movie "Game of Thrones" then behind the throne is a seven-pointed star showing everyone worshipped seven Gods, and seven kingdoms. There was but one God and one Goddess, the rest were their children or Angels, different cultures, different civilizations called them by different names, we all know this, and the rest are children, yes, sons and daughter of this God and Goddess. So now, you ask who were these other five? We know long before Jesus was born and the New Testament was written and long before Moses was born and the Old Testament was written, long before Adam and Eve and this world was created, it would be safe to say in the beginning there was a male entity and a female entity. We call them God and Goddess. Does our God have a male penis and a pair of balls? Does our

Goddess have a vagina and a pair of tits? Do they have fingerprints, like we do? They got together and created children, the same way they created us to do and the first born was lucifer, The light. I believe lucifer had both the male and female anatomy and occasionally, that does happen so this God and Goddess adjusted everything and created a daughter, they called her Auriel, some call Her Uriel without the A. If we think of lucifer as the first prodigal son, then could our Auriel be the first prodigal daughter? Did she too rebell? We call her mother earth or mother nature, did our creators give Her this world to rule over? we know a lot of children were born and we call them Angels.do these male angels have a penis and balls? We know in Genesis chapter six it talks about the sons of God came down and saw the daughters of men were beautiful and they TOOK them wives, Did the woman have a choice? they said there was giants in the land so did these offspring become these giants? Was Hercules a giant from God and a mortal female? Can there be others? We know goliath was a giant and there were many other giants, were did they come from?   Do these female angels have a vagina and a pair of tits? Did they create these baby angels or cherubs we call them? Do these baby angels ever grow up and become teenage angels? do they later get married and have baby cherub angels? Do they have fingerprints also? Do they have wings? I do not know; can they fly around? I do not know, maybe we just think that for a bird to get here then they have to fly here, so if an angel shows up then they would have to have wings and fly here, again I do not know. We do know a third of the angels, led by lucifer, decided to rebell, why? How many years were they here? How many angels were in this rebellion? We know a third of the angels led by Lucifer, the 1st born decided to rebell because they wanted to rule over something. God got mad and either broke their wings   Then did our God decided to create humans in our Image in the image of us and give

these humans something for these rebellious
angels to rule over? We do know after God did
create Adam and Eve God, then he did stand
back and watched, and the bible says God looked
down and saw all the evil that was created and
decided to destroy everything with a flood. We all
know about Genesis, we also know they did not
have cameras and books written, so all this was
handed down from one generation to another."
End of lecture seminar end of chapter 4 scene 4

Reflections

I look in the Mirror, and what do I see,
nothing but a stranger looking back at me,
when I was young, and saw my face,
I laughed and played, without a trace,
of fear or doubt of what I would be,
gray hair and wrinkles starring back at me,
I searched for wisdom, I searched for knowledge,
but I never found it in ay school or college,
the bible I read from cover to cover,
the books I read, I would only discover,
there is more to life, than meets the eye,
If we search our heart, ask the reason why,
sometimes we search all our lives to find,
that each human being is a one of a kind,
even Molecules, atoms, protons and more,
if you could think and add up the score,
the answer you seek you may never find,
the parable, the puzzle, that freaks the mind,
you look in the Mirror and what do you see,
only the best you turn out to be   copyright 2006
www.poetry.com by Melvin Abercrombie

act five scene five

The old man is talking " I know I said this before
but needs to be repeated, If you break the Law,
they will arrest you, then Fingerprint you to find
out who you are. You will stand before a Judge
with over a hundred levels of punishment
according to what level you done, as a Christian
you were taught, you only get to live one lifetime
and stand before the Judge with only two
Levels?? Heaven or hell forever and ever? All we

know is what we were taught, all they can teach us is what they were taught. What if they were taught wring? Someone is right someone is wrong, who gets to decide? This world has been around a long time, from a cave man to who we are today. Long ago everything was passed down by word of the mouth from one generation to the next, finally thru the years we figured out how to carve words on a stone and eventually create paper. I believe Auriel, the 1st born daughter was not a part of the rebellion, so our God and Goddess gave her this world to rule over and we still to this day call her Mother Earth or Mother Nature." he paused for a break and Brigitte got up to ask him a question "Did you actually study Wicca?" Yes, he said, and I know you, bill and veronica have too, as a male witch we like to call our self a Warlock so that is what me and Bill like to use. I also have gone thru the 5 Initiations of the temple of Vampires" yes she smiled "I thought when I first met you that you were a kindred spirit, a very old soul" yes he replied I felt your energy when you uncrossed your legs to show me you have no panties on, you are very beautiful and very tempting but you see my wife, so I got more than I can handle, so can we all be more professional and get this all on film?" yes she smiled i will let you finish your seminar lecture" the old man went back to the microphone and continued " We also know God did divide the world up into four directions, north was given to Auriel, mother earth and if you go clockwise then east was given to Raphael or the air spirit. south was given to Michael, the fire spirit and west was given to Gabriel, she rules over the water. Lucifer was the light and because of his rebellion he was cast out and rules the sun as the 1st born son. We think of the sun as good and there is good in lucifer, but also if you try to get into a rocket ship and land on the sun you will be burned up. We now know the sun is a ball of fire that evolves around the earth, or the earth evolves around the sun. So now if you accept the original male god, Yahweh and the goddess, Shekinah, then Lucifer,

Auriel, Raphael, Michael and Gabriel then you have the original 7 Gods, the olde world did worship. We know thru the years our male attitude did not want a female as equal so we created these all male religions, Christianity, Islam, buddha and Jewish and divided and scattered and confused we have different religions like hundred Christian labels, some different Jewish and Islam and then buddha and the Hindu religions, so you see lucifer been very busy laughing his butt off at how stupid and easy to manipulate these mortal, temporary, flesh and blood human beings are not knowing they have this secret to Immortality, then finally God, knowing he was getting old and going to die, sent Jesus down to help straighten out this world and what happened? Was God very old? Did God and the Goddess die? we want to think of God as a long gray hair and a long gray beard during the time of Moses that was what Moses saw back then, over 2,000 years ago. Actually Jesus was trying to teach these 8 truths or secrets, the Jewish rabbi people in charge did not like this because they did not want a female to have the same power any-more, so when our God and goddess did die and time did change from bc to ad and lucifer took over because he was the first born son and he did not want his younger brother Jesus, this new upstart to take over, lucifer waited thousands of years for this day and he earned it, so lucifer made sure they, the Jewish rabbi's, had him killed to silence him.. So now, that is enough of that, let's talk about another cool story. When I was a child, we would go to my mother's grandparents' house on weekends. Grandpa was olde skool Irish, he believed in a God, Cerrunos and a Goddess, Cerridwen, He was Celtic, red hair and lots of freckles but now old and gray. grandma was Cherokee Indian, she was taught along the same lines of equality, her religion was father sky and mother earth. My mom and dad were good Christian Baptist that is how they were taught and tried to change grandpa and grandma, but they stuck to the olde religion all their life. I remember one day setting on the porch it was raining and grandma looked up at the rain then looked at me and said, Melvin, did you know that the angels look down and they see all the evil and mean things mankind has done and they start to cry. So, when you see it raining then all the angels are crying. This I remember now almost sixty years later so sometimes when it rains, I think about my grandpa and grandma and the old porch swing and the simple life they lived. I remember lots of other stories they shared with me and always told me to ask questions and do not give up until you get the right answers. This book and movie, Avalon Fishermen Church is about some of those stories I have told some before in other books some need to be repeated again and again. Now on my father's side of the family tree, grandpa was German, or so i thought, the Abercrombie name is a Scottish name. I stop, take a drink of water and so I go on, " It seems now adays everyone is coming out of the closet. you have gay people tired of hiding and now openly tell everyone that they are a man who likes another man or now lesbians who say they are a man trapped in a woman's body and like woman or both. so welcome to free America. I am still a male during this lifetime and still love the female species so that way I am normal. I see black men marrying white woman and having half breed babies that are beautiful and normal today. Same with Hispanic and oriental inter breeding, so now it's open season. What if a day will come when we will no longer have labels and category dividing us? Yes, we have rich billionaires talking about this new age movement called the new world order and I think back, maybe they too are looking at the big picture wrong, what if they should call it the olde world order. Maybe we need to go back to when Adam and eve were around and we did have one God and one Goddess, we had one church, one language, one religion, one Brotherhood, and all the people understood everything and were not scattered and confused. So, do angels still look down and see all the evil and mean people all over the world and do they cry? When it rains is this the angels crying? Yes, I have lived many lifetimes and I will talk about some of these hidden in all this you could say I was taught wicca or did understand and love the mother earth we were given. so, a male type species would not want to be called a witch or a male witch that does not sound masculine yes, we understood evil and good, it's not just one or the other there are a hundred shades of good and another hundred shades of evil so to me i love the idea of being a warlock, or a male witch. But then I grew up loving a male God and a Jesus Christ as the son of our God. so, to me there must be equality. what if we join the female Goddess wicca and the male Christian God together? We will talk about that again later, but we do know there is a movement were the Christian wicca is being created, is this good or bad? Do we eventually have a Jewish wicca? An Islam Wicca? Or maybe a Buddha Wicca? Do we need another religion out there? I know I have lived many lifetimes. Now I understand this gift of Immortality we all have believe it or not, I remember a partial recall sometimes thru self-Hypnosis and some things are crystal clear. I am also a real vampyre and we will talk about that also not just what you see in Hollywood as a blood sucking Dracula to scare little children. Most people do not understand what a real vampyre really is. most people do not understand what a real warlock really is. I worship a male God I call Yahweh, yes, He has a wife, I call her Shekinah, she is the Goddess, the queen of heaven. I believe and teach the real Jesus Christ, the Ha Mashiach, the Messiah that very few really know. I am not special, just a kid asking a lot of what if questions and not giving up so yes, I am a male witch, or what we would call a Warlock. I cast my circle of protection, but I do a full 360-degree full permanent circle or bubble, surrounding me and my family and loved ones. I open my circle calling upon my male God, Yahweh and the female Goddess, Shekinah to

come into my circle and give me their protection,
then i face in the north direction which is earth I
respect mother nature, she is Auriel, the first born
daughter, yes mother earth and I call upon her for
protection then just like any other wiccan I go
clock wise, deosil to the east direction and call
upon Raphael, the air spirit, then go south and
call upon the fire spirit, Michael then west which
is water and she is Gabriel. then complete my
circle of protection but I keep my circle around me
24/7/365 all the time. Now you understand a little
about the warlock side of me as equality. What if
the real vampyre is not drinking blood but drinking
the energy or lifeforce from other spirits? What is
the Einstein code about? This E=MC2 mean? Are
we all not just energy beings? Yes, immortal
energy beings, that is what Immortality is all
about, we are stuck in a temporary, flesh and
blood, mortal body so we can experience, feed,
drink, so we can create more energy? We do not
kill anyone, I can use my five senses and can
draw your energy from you, sort of like a vacuum
cleaner sucks up the dust, everyone knows the
five senses, Seeing, hearing, touch, taste and
smell, so I have learned to use these 5 senses to
absorb your energy from you and as my lover or
wife, I can draw her orgasm, which is the nectar
of the Gods, the creation process. I can drink that
instead of blood, taste a lot better and she gives
willingly. Has anyone ever thought that originally,
all of God and Goddess children were all angels?
We know that lucifer was the first-born son of this
God and Goddess and was the first rebel angel.
We also know that lucifer convinced a third of His
brothers and sisters to join him and they started
the rebellion that got them kicked out of heaven
and now are called demons, how many of these
fallen demons are male and how many are
female? How many of the other two thirds called
angels are male angels and how many are
female angels? so what is your definition of a
demon? what is your definition of a angel? We
were taught that everything is a dual nature, the
first wisdom we learn is called duality and the

symbol is a coin showing there are only two sides
of everything, up-down, left-right, male-female,
forward-back-ward, good -evil, so is everything
black or white? Can there be a hundred shades
of red? where do we draw the line from being a
angel to being a demon? If God can forgive us of
our sins and give us another chance can God
give these demons another chance? We all know
the bible story were a third of the Angels were
cast out of heaven, where did these fallen angels
go to? Where are they now? Could there be
angels and demons among us today? If God and
Goddess created everything then does that mean
we all are sons and daughters of them? some of
my other books I use the scenario of what if
Lucifer was tired of playing the bad guy and
finally wanted to settle down, and get married,
have children, will God and goddess forgive him?
If God can forgive us then can God forgive
lucifer? can lucifer say the 3 magic words, God
forgive me will God forgive him? When we pray,
we pray to "Our father who art in heaven
hallowed be thy name, thy kingdom come, thy will
be done on earth as it is in heaven" and if you are
a Christian, you end your prayer in Jesus' name,
right? What If Jesus Christ is the son of God, then
would that make Jesus an angel? In Genesis
chapter six, the sons of God looked down and
saw the daughters of man were beautiful and
took them wives and there were giants in the
land, did these angels able to pro create like we
do? we see pictures and statues of baby angels
so do these baby angels grow up to be teenager
angels? then get married and have more baby
angels? what if the female angels come down
and have sex with the sons of god can they
create giants too? So, does that mean like
Hercules who was half god, and half mortal
female then why was Jesus not a giant? We do
know that lucifer did take Jesus up on the
mountain and did all kinds of test and brought him
back down and said "surely this is the son of
God" so does that mean that Jesus and lucifer
are brothers? Is lucifer a giant also? are all

angels giant compared to us mortals? When we pray, we pray to our father and end our prayer in Jesus' name so is God our father also? Is Jesus our brother? That means lucifer is also our brother, right? So, if lucifer is the first rebel angel then what Jesus did would he be called a rebel angel also? We know for a fact the roman leader at the time, Pilate, did not want to kill this Jewish, rebel leader named Jesus Christ, He even washed his hands of the whole matter. The Jewish rabbis were adamant in wanting Jesus dead to silence him. Did they find out this Jesus, they allowed to be a Rabbi, was not ever circumcised, would God allow His son to be changed? What gives us the right to change what our God, our creator did create? The Jewish rabbis were even willing to let a known murderer go free so Jesus would be killed to silence Him. What was Jesus teaching that was so bad they had to kill him to silence him? Did the Jewish rabbi think of Jesus as a rebel? We know Jesus believed in equality, yes, a male God and a female Goddess, the Hebrew called their male God Yahweh, and the female Goddess was called Shekinah, queen of heaven. The romans had no problem with that, they spoke a different language and called their God Jupiter and their Goddess Juno. We also know two or three hundred years after our Jesus was killed, the Romans were still persecuting these new Christians and in 313ad the Roman leader Constantine finally made a decree to change the 7th day Saturday Jewish day of rest to a Sunday, the 1st day of the week, why? the people were taking off work two days instead of just one. The romans did not care what day you take off as long as you work six days and get things done. The new Christians chose Sunday, the 1st day of the week because that was the day Christ arose from the grave, even in his death Christ was a Jewish person and kept the 7th day Saturday sabbath. Constantine was more in favor to the Christians and the Roman Empire started the Roman Catholic Church. They changed their God Jupiter

to the now Christian God Jehovah and took their
Goddess Juno and believed she was the Holy
Ghost that Luke was talking about that went into
the Virgin Mary, so Jesus could be born. So now
the Goddess Juno became the Virgin Mary,
Mother of our Lord and Savior, the only son of
God during this time. Did God marry the virgin,
Mary? No, she was already promised to Joseph.
Did God break his own laws of Deuteronomy22?
Why would God, the father allows Joseph,
knowing he was from the right bloodline of the
tribe of Judah, the lion of Judah then not use
him? Luke tells us that a Angel told joseph to not
lay with his wife. What angel has the power to
defy God's laws? Only Lucifer but is this what
really happened? What If this Angel told Joseph
to not lay with the virgin Mary, then were they
ever actually legally married? For a Marriage to
be legal a husband and wife must sleep together
Those who did not agree with this new Roman
Catholic church did protest and we call these
Protestors, the Protestant church which became
the Baptist, Methodist, Mormon, Presbyterian,
Church of God, Church of Christ, Lutheran and
many other offspring denominations. Have you
ever wondered why we, as a Christian nation,
now believing in a Male God, a new male son of
this God and another male we call the Holy Spirit,
but no one knows who that third male actually is?
The only other male in this creation process has
to be the original rebel angel, Lucifer himself but
no one wants you to know this, so they hid this
from you and then put a female statue of a
Goddess on top of our white house capitol were
our President and Congress meet? Seems to me
if we have a Christian Trinity as our new religion,
we will maybe put a male statue of a male God
up there. You know with a long beard and robe
showing the world, we worship a male God type
entity? We now have over a hundred different
Christian religions all saying we have a Trinity
showing we worship a male type God, a new
male son of this God as Jesus Christ and another
male entity we all call a male Holy Spirit but no

one really knows who that third entity actually is.so it looks to me like there is a lot of rebellion going on one church not liking another church so they rebell against them and start their own church, over and over again, looks like we have a lot of rebel angels going around. We also have a huge female statue of a Goddess type person in our harbor in New York showing the Statue of Liberty, a female as the symbol of the United States of America, we also call this world Mother Earth or Mother Nature, the Greeks called her Persephone but again, we no longer worship a female in this creation process, why? We do know that when our Jesus Christ was alive and did walk this earth many cultures, many civilizations did worship a male God and a female Goddess as equal. The Romans were the ones who nailed our Jesus on the cross, but they were forced to kill this rebel angel because the Jewish Rabbi's at this time knew they had to silence him, so do not blame the Romans for killing our Rebel Angel, blame the Jewish Rabbi who had their own little rebellion going on. The Jewish Rabbi's did not want to no longer worship a female as equal and other religions followed that decree like the Buddha and Islam, so they had their little rebellion going on against anyone who did believe in this equality. The Romans believed in a male God, they called Jupiter and a female Goddess they called Juno. You can go to Rome Italy today and still see the remnants the statues of the Goddess, we call that the Olde Religion. The Egyptians, called their God Osiris and their Goddess was known as Isis and you can still go to Egypt today and still see the remnants, the temples of Isis and the statues of the Goddess. We can go on, the Greeks, called their male God Zeus and their Goddess was known as Hera and you can go to the Greek Islands and still see the Remnants, the statues and why of all the different Goddess statues to pick from would we, the United States of America pick the Goddess Persephone or mother earth as the one we want on top of our white house capitol building for everyone to see forever and ever? We also know a long time ago most of Europe was divided into two groups the Celtic, England, Scotland, Wales and Ireland had their God as Cerrunos and their Goddess was called Cerridwen. The Vikings, Germany and Scandinavian countries were called Teutonic, their God was called Odin and their Goddess was known as Freya. they called their heaven Valhalla, the place you go to in your afterlife. So, you see many different countries, speaking a different language worshipping a male God and a female Goddess as equal while Jesus Christ was alive walking around on this earth, just two thousand years ago. Remember Moses was saved by the daughter of the Egyptian Pharoah, he was taught the religion of the Egyptians of Isis. In many ways we could say Moses was a rebellious person. we know he had the power to turn a walking stick into a snake and eat another snake so when we think of a snake what rebel angel do, we think of? We also know that the same Moses was talking to a burning bush on fire so when we think of fire what rebel angel do, we think of? We also know in the beginning, long before Jesus Christ was born and the new testament was written, long before Moses was born and the old testament was written, long before Adam and eve were created and this world was created there was one male God and one female Goddess, there was one church, one Religion, we call it the olde world order Now the Goddess returns" The old man stops and walks off the stage Brigitte and the film crew wrap everything up and are ready for more drinks and wild times back at the mansion. his two bodyguards surround him, yes, a big cowboy and a Japanese woman, that later on you will see she is a modern female, Bruce Lee. This time she looks at the camera and as they walk, she does the talking" The lecture was a good one, a lot of people left, still not satisfied at all this Da Vinci Code crap. I saw the movie and read all dan browns books and I can see there is a bigger world out there beside my Buddha, so is my

Buddha our God? This is what I was taught and me and this old fart redneck cowboy here have been talking about this for the last five years. I have given a little and listened to his belief system and He has learned a little Buddha We have learned to fall in Love with each other, but we try not to let it show, always professional, doing our job and protecting our boss." The cowboy opens the door to the Rolls Royce and the old man and his wife, gets in, they look and notice Brigitte and the film crew are already loading up and heading back to the mansion for some more fun, they look around and both get in and drive off, The next scene is at the ocean front mansion, body guards at the gate and around the perimeter, the old man setting in his favorite chair taking a drink, his wife, and a group of friends setting around, the camera crew is filming everything and Brigette watching as the old man speaks: "We want to believe that our Christian Jesus Christ is the only son of a male God. then who created Lucifer? Sometimes I say the same thing over and over again, this is how you remember thru repetitions. Remember long before Jesus was born and long before the New Testament was written, long before Moses was born and the Old Testament was written, long before Adam and eve and this world was created. there were a male God and a female goddess, and they had many children, we call them angels, actually the first-born generation were called arch angels and the first-born son was called Lucifer, but we want to think of lucifer as a wicked male with horns and a pitchfork. we know they had a rebellion and a third of these angels were cast out of heaven. where did they go? Was lucifer the first prodigal son? Did he ever ask the father for forgiveness? If he did would our father forgive him? Was Auriel a part of the original third of the Angels rebellion? Was She the first Prodigal daughter? We do know our creator, Father and Mother did give this earth to Auriel to rule as a Mother Earth or a Mother Nature we will talk about that again and again. I have this dream,

when we die, we all get to go to a heaven forever
and ever and we will see this one church, one
religion, we think we will never grow old but when
you see baby Angels, either pictures or statues
and you call these baby angels, Cherubs, do they
ever grow up? Do they become teenage angels?
then maybe young adults who eventually will get
married and have the same power that God and
the Goddess gave us and that is to create a new
life? New baby Angels? Do we never grow old in
heaven? We think of God as a old gray hair man
with a long gray beard so is God old? Does He
ever die like us and go into a new life form and
start over? If God did die and Lucifer is the first-
born son then is Lucifer ruling this world now? Is
this why we changed time from B.C. to A.D. we
want to think that our Jesus Christ had a lot to do
with that but if you look at all the different
Religions of the World, very few actually knew
this man of 33 years old who died a horrible
death nailed to a cross so a known murderer go
free? So, the first rebel angel, Lucifer, the real
first-born son of our God and Goddess, who led a
third of his brothers and sister angels in a
rebellion and created a lot more rebel angels, but
we want to now call them demons? Are they
demons or rebel angels? When we, as mortal
Humans ask God to forgive us of our sins then
are they, as demons, entitled to the same
forgiveness? We are scattered and confused for
sure. We will talk about this again ,Dinner is being
served for all that is hungry I will do my morning
walk along the beach, be right back" end of
chapter five scene five

One plus one equals

one   I close my eyes and come to
you,   we are in the
forest, the sky is blue
you are my Goddess, my Queen, my love,
God has given me to you, from up above,
He heard my prayers, He felt my pain,
He knows my sorrow, and you I shall gain,

to pull me out of this quicksand of doubt,
The turbulence troubles, and turn me about,
A new man He has made me away from this
strife,   the evil, the dangers, the
madness of life,   there is a light
at the end of the night,
sometimes we can't see it and we lose sight,
of the things that are precious, the taste of a tear,
the things we are afraid of, we mostly will fear,
we go thru life, never to understand,
the value of a woman, the price of a man,
who decides what a body is worth,
only our God can tell us, from the time of our
birth,   Each day we decide what path we
will take,   and which road we
choose, is it a mistake?   I
can close my eyes and come to you,
we are in the forest, the sky is blue.   copyright
2006   www.poetry.com Melvin Abercrombie

Act six scene six

Ocean front mansion, walking on the beach,   the
sexy voice continues" His wife, loves to walk with
them on the beach she has her shorts on , loose
blouse and towel around her waist, big straw hat
and sunglasses and camera zooms in on all of
them including Brigitte wearing her little bitty
bikini, The scene is a typical ocean, sandy beach,
it is early morning, yes, we are very rich, yes we
have our own ocean front property, Brigette, the
two camera crew, Bill and veronica filming and
His two guards, Rex and Jasmine, escort them
around for his usual morning walk. He likes to
walk barefoot, toes in the sand, pants rolled up a
little and the ocean waves splashing on his feet,
off in a distance the sun rises over the ocean, the
sound of seagulls could be heard, the two guards
are always looking in all directions, there job is to
protect this rich old couple at all cost, yes even
taking a bullet for them if they have to, they hear
the old man talking to himself, they are used to it,
whatever angels or demons He is talking to does
not matter, they laugh among themselves,
smiling, they to enjoy the morning walk. The old

man steps on something and stops, she laughs at
how the maids are always saying the things they
find in his pockets like a little 7-year-old kid nails,
snails' parts of a seashell you never know what
you will find in his pockets", smiling she
continues: " is it just another partial seashell or?
He pauses and bends over to see something
shiny and picks it up to find a old brass Aladdin
lamp, as he wipes off the sand a Genie appears,
she notices it but says nothing, the guards,
Brigitte, and film crew do not see the genie, only
the old couple, as he continues walking, holding
the Aladdin lamp tightly, He goes back into time
as a child and says " i remembers when I was a
Kid and the genie would give me three wishes
and over and over I would think, what would I
really wish for? Knowing the rules, I knew I had to
be careful of what you say, if you ask for a million
bucks you may wound up with a million male
deer, so the words, once said cannot be
reversed, then you cannot ask for two or more
things, so be careful and not use the word AND.
Then I realized what if the Genie was already
gone? what if this was just a toy lamp and I rub it
and nothing happens?" The genie was watching
him and politely says" I am real, yes you found
me, and the problem is, the last person already
used up two of the wishes, so now you will only
get one wish. Once you open your mouth,
whatever you say will be your wish and this wish
will only be granted if you unscrew the lid and
throw the lid in the ocean as for as you can, this
will free me, and your one wish will be granted.
Keep the lid and I will remain trapped inside and
you will not get your wish. It is your choice." the
old man continues walking and thinking about
what the one wish would be, she realizes what is
going on and he only gets one wish so she
cannot say anything out loud, but she can talk to
the camera crew and Brigitte to tell them to film
this and be really quiet. as she takes several
steps back and let them walk ahead the camera
zooms in on her now " yes if he had three wishes,
one would be for twenty million dollars, but now

he already has that much money, so money would not be a wish. a long time ago He wanted his second wish to be a long life. What good is having lots of money, if you die the next week? Now he is old, yes, he has lived a long life, so he would not wish for that. His third wish would have been a healthy/ disease free life, what good is millions of dollars and a long life if you are sick with a disease? He realizes God has blessed him with a healthy disease-free life, so this too has been granted. So, the three things he would have wished for, He already has been granted. He says a short prayer thankful for all that has been given him. He remembers reading the Holy Bible and in 1Kings, of the Old Testament, Solomon was visited by an angel and granted one wish, what did he wish for? An understanding heart, " his wife catches up with them and looks at her husband with knowing eyes, does not say a word, He knows that she knows, and they smile and Yes, the old man hollers out loud "Grant me this understanding heart." The two guards were surprised, smiling they all continued, not seeing this genie and then seeing the old man toss the lid of the Aladdin lamp far into the ocean, the guards just think it was a rock or something he picked up. The genie says, "very wise wish and I think you for freeing me, now your wish will be granted, keep the lamp as a souvenir, place it on your fireplace mantle so you will be reminded, now I am gone." the sexy voice continues "the old man puts the Lamp in His pocket and they all head back to their mansion, ready for their morning coffee and breakfast. as they all head to the table" the camera zooms in on his wife, and she says " Yes, now he has this Understanding heart, it is time to share this wisdom and knowledge with the world. Those who are ready will understand, yes, he will write many books, the olde Law TO Know, To Dare, Remain Silent, Will be now To Know, To Dare, To Teach. Then after he has said what needs to be said, He must again, go back to the olde law and remain silent. It is time for the world to know the truths, In the beginning there was 1 church, one religion. In the end the world will go back to this one church, one religion. It will be called Avalon Fishermen church Ministry. millions of people will buy his books, not because he wrote them, but because they now teach the truths, now with this understanding heart he can explain things to them and they too will understand and know these truths" the sexy voice continues ", The film shows various scenes of the old man eating and the usual daytime activities, all the friends leave, only the ghost camera see's everything then the old man goes up stairs to bed, yes an exciting day he has waited all his life for this one day to finally get this understanding heart why was it not given a long time ago? He keeps saying what if, when he could have helped so many other people, these thoughts going thru his head as he prepares for sleep, lights out, the mansion is in shut down mode. Rex and Jasmine go to their quarters next to each other and they can unlock the door that separates them or if they want privacy then one will lock their side. Movie producers and others reading this book can imagine wild sex scenes where they both take a shower together or?? Camera goes to a new scene, not the camera bill and veronica has for the Hollywood gossip, they are still sleeping but the real movie camera scene: your typical Bedroom, the light thru the window curtain showing a early morning sun peeking in just enough light to see the old couple sleeping in the bed, the alarm goes off, a hand comes out of the cover to silence the loud alarm clock, as He reaches for the alarm button you see the Hand and arm shapeshift into a demonic being with long fingernails only for a moment, was this just a movie camera trick? He silences the alarm and the hand shifts back to normal. She rolls over and goes back to sleep, let him go do this by his self, this time, she has things she needs to do anyway. The old man gets out of the bed, wearing his favorite red plaid flannel pajamas, he walks over to the light switch and reaches out to turn the bedroom light on again, as his hand reaches out, only for a moment, it again shape shifts into this demonic hand with long fingernails, only for a moment and he turns the bedroom light on. The camera shows the old man walking to the bathroom, again, is this the same as a long time ago could this happen to him again? He thinks to himself wondering if he will again fly thru the air, what can he do to stop this madness? Go back to sleep? then as he again reaches around the door to turn on the bathroom light, again his hand shape-shifts into this demonic finger with long curly fingernails only for a moment, as he turns on the light. He looks in the mirror and says to himself, "Looks like I need a shave" He goes thru the drawers and cabinets to get shaving cream, razor blade, toothpaste and toothbrush, as he looks in the mirror, the camera zooms in on his eyes and they turn glossy black, showing now the demonic spirit has completely entered the old man's body. Smiling he again reaches in the drawer for his scissor and starts cutting all his hair off, gobs of gray hair fall all over the bathroom counter, then he shakes the shaving cream up and gobs it all over his head and shaves all his hair off except his cool handle-bar moustache and eye brows, He grabs a wash cloth, wipes excess off, takes off his pajamas, naked, he looks down at his limp uncircumcised penis and says out loud to no one "I am a uncircumcised gentile, not worthy to be a Jewish person like my Jesus" with tears in his eyes he again looks down and says " I remember he used to stand up and watch me shave, now he just watches me tie my shoes". he opens the shower curtain, turns on the water, goes into the shower, camera scans around the room at all the fallen gray hair all over the place, the sound of the shower stopping, the camera goes back to see the old man Open the Shower Curtain. Out walks a Younger Version of the Old man, now with tattoos all over his chest and upper arms, He reaches for a towel to dry off and raises his hands in the air shouting "Now I feel the power" as he says this two four feet long black demonic wings appear on his back and start flapping, smiling he rises from the ground, camera shows his feet off the ground as he flies around in the bathroom. Out of nowhere a loud thunder and lightning hits his right wing and you hear the snap, as the wing is broken, you see his face, the pain as he falls to the floor and curls up, camera zooms in on his back, as blood pours out, you can see the broken wing, as He sobs uncontrollable "my God forgive me, my Goddess forgive me, Jesus Christ forgive me" he cries out to no avail, curled up, sobbing on the floor, the camera shows the two wings slowly fade away and disappear. All the blood slowly fades away and disappears, only a naked, old man lay there, crying. After a while the crying stops, as he reaches up to pull himself up on the bathroom counter, once again, you see His hand shape-shift into this demonic hand then his other hand reaches up to pull himself up and again you see his other hand shapeshift only for a moment, He grabs a towel to dry off and wipe away his tears, as he looks in the mirror, He notices all the tattoo's and cries out "Why? Is this the Mark of the Beast?" He grabs a washcloth and tries to wash away the tattoos to no avail, they are permanent. He slowly puts his clothes back on, brushes his teeth, reaches for the comb to comb his hair, then remembers He has none, He combs his handlebar moustache. smiling he starts to walk out of the bathroom, as he reaches out to turn the light off, he pauses in midair, smiling again, He twirls his fingers and the lights go off, yes, he still has some powers, now how do you control It? If my hands turn to a demonic being will other parts of me change? these thoughts going thru his head as he walks down the staircase. Rex and Jasmine are at the bottom to greet him, and the cowboy says, "Wow What in thunder happened to you?" The old man smiles, as he walks down the steps and Jasmine says yes, you look ten years younger," Laughing she says: " you trying to look like our Buddha?" Smiling, the old man says" "No actually I had a demonic possession episode and now I have all these tattoos all over my chest and now I need to go see my pagan friend the High Priestess, I was involved with her a long time ago back in my hippie days" Then the butler said, "your wife not going?" he replies, "No she has some woman errand's, her bridge club, beauty shop etc.," they smile and go to the lecture hall it was a great two hour lecture on the other secrets of the Holy Grail and lots of people will buy the books, Rex speaks: " now we will escort him to see this High Priestess, Jasmine found her phone number and address and set up an appointment to be discreet not a lot of people around so now we are driving him there to see why he has all these tattoos on him now., as we pull up Jasmine says "You stay here I will go inside make sure everything is ok" Nodding and taking his sun glasses off he looks in the rear view mirror at the old man in the back seat and says "Sir just a precaution" He smiling looks around and says "Yes thank you" Jasmine comes out showing every-thing is ok, she looks around and opens the door for him to get out and he is escorted in. She stands by the door in case someone else wants to come in and Rex and the old man sees the High Priestess. The camera zooms back to Jasmine at the door, and she says:" what you do not know but our job is to check out and protect him and we saw they were more than friends a long time ago, actually they were lovers, and He was the High Priest Himself going thru all 3 Initiations of Wicca and the 5 Initiations of Temple of Vampires." Smiling she nods her head and says, "Just so you know" then the camera goes back to the High Priestess who says, "Melvin Merlyne Merlyne what have you been up to? it's been twenty years since I see you and I heard you are doing ok" He replied smiling "Yes not bad How about You?" Smiling back, she says "I miss the Old days, heard you are trying to go back to this Old religion trying to join your Christian God to our Goddess, don't you know people have been trying to do that for thousands of years?" He sets down and removes his shirt saying "I have to show you something, I

woke up with all these tattoos on and I wondered
where they came from" She looks at all the
tattoos and frowns, realizing he is losing his
memory with sad eyes she sets down next to him
and says "Melvin, Merlyne Merlyne you have had
all these same tattoos for over thirty years, you
were a bad ass biker guy who was a crazy
asshole who fighting your demons, you thought
you could control them with drugs and alcohol
and when we met I taught you the reason for
each one of these tattoos you got but did not
know why, don't you remember?" The old man
looked up as rex and jasmine walked in and saw
the same tattoos he had on forever and they too
realized he was slowly losing his mind. She
points at the six pointed star of David and says
"Remember the male symbol is a upright Triangle
and the female symbol is a upside down triangle"
Yes he says I do remember and you added the
Christian cross in the middle showing you love
the teachings of the Christ and this was your
symbol for our Goddess her nipple is your nipple
she rules over your Heart don't you remember
that?" slowly he remembers each tattoo and what
they represented and he realized it was just the
demonic forces playing a game on him he pays
her well and now back home to another day he
asked his guards to not say anything to his wife
about this or his tattoos they all know he had
them for at least thirty years just getting old "
Another scene, another story Brigitte and the
camera crew has arrived for their daily filming as
his wife speaks " I was still amazed at why he cut
off all his gray hair, yes he does look a lot
younger I go to the beauty shop and pay
hundreds to hide this gray and he does it for free
"smiling she says " so everyone goes into the
great living room and all get a drink, Casual and
settle down. The butler fixes them their favorite
margarita with the little umbrella and cherry. the
old man, as tradition takes the stem and gives me
the cherry and I give him my cherry he takes a
drink and smiling he starts the third secret:"
"Jesus did teach Re-incarnation, He asked His

disciples, "Who do people say I am? one of them replied "Some say you are Elijah" How can Jesus be Elijah who died a long time ago, a different face, different hair and eyes and a different finger-print or was it? Then another story says Jesus is the word and the word was with us from the beginning so could our Jesus be a re-incarnation of Adam? Did Adam just die and is in the ground waiting on this future Resurrection that Paul talks about in Corinthians and Thessalonians? Paul mentions the graves will give up the dead and the oceans will give up the dead and those alive will be caught up in a twinkling of an eye and all will be Judged at this one great throne judgement day? Do we just live one life and everyone is judged and either go to a Heaven or a hell forever and ever? does that make sense? Can you experience everything you would like to Experience in only one lifetime? Can you ask God to give you another chance, you did not get to Experience everything you wanted to Experience in only one lifetime? another story They were walking along and saw a man born blind, one disciple said "was this a sin from the Parents? It was obvious he was born blind so it could not be some sin he did during this lifetime. They believed in the afterlIfe, yes, each life you die, and your physical mortal, flesh and blood body does go back to the ground and your spirit/soul is judged, yes, every knee shall bow, yes, every tongue shall confess, each life you are judged, and God gives you another chance at this game called life. you do not get to go to a heaven forever and ever. does that make sense? No what do you do up there for an eternity? Can you get married? Have Children? do Angels and demons have babies? Do they have a fingerprint? I wrote a book called Fingerprint and I went into detail talking just about that one subject. My first book written long ago by Trafford publishing I asked the question Does God Have a Penis? The publishing company loved the idea and asked me to go to Orlando Florida for a book signing and give me 5o free books to autograph and give away to help promote the advertisement with big signs and lots of people, I sold out fast, I only had about a hundred book markers they gave me, and I signed them to the rest of the crowd. So, you ask, is God a male? Is the Goddess, Shekinah, a female? Are they male and female angels and demons? Why would Moses say in Genesis that Adam and eve were created in our Image, in the Image of us? If God did all this by his self, would he not say he created Adam and eve In my image in the image of me or as a singular phrase? If you read in Genesis chapter three, God was walking in the garden of Eden and He was looking for Adam and eve, He could not see them, so he hollers out "Where are you at?" Adam stuck his head out of the bushes and replied, "We were hiding because we were naked" God replied, "Did you eat from the forbidden tree I told you not too?" Adam replied, eve did, and she made me do it" Did eve pull out a 44-magnum pistol, like clint Eastwood and say make my day punk and made him eat the forbidden apple? No Adam had a choice, but Adam chose to eat and blamed it on eve, it was her fault. Even in the beginning man did not want to accept responsibility. it is easier to blame someone else. So now the questions, If God was walking in the garden of Eden does God have one leg? Two legs, three legs or four legs? Does God have thighs, kneecaps, ankles feet, toes and toenails? We want to think we, as mortal, flesh and blood temporary humans are created in the image of God so we have two legs so God must have two legs also, right? Now God was looking for Adam and eve, right? so does God have one, two three or four eyes? How many eyes does God have? Remember in school, science, physical science or biology you studied the eyeball and had to name all the different parts and you had a test with a picture of this eyeball with all these different arrows showing each part, like this was the pupil, this was the cornea, this was the retina and way back in the back was the optic nerve, remember? So now does God have

blue, green, brown or what color eyes? Does God
have eye lashes and eyebrows? are they gray
like his beard and long gray hair to show God is
very Old? Does God ever cry with real tears?
Grandma used to tell me that when it rains it was
all the angels crying because they looked down
and saw all the evil going on in this world. If God
was talking to Adam, then does God have a
tongue? Lips and teeth? If God is very old, does
he have false teeth and takes them out at night
and puts them in a jar of water like grandpa used
to do? We were told from the Baptist preacher
that grandpa is up in heaven with Jesus right now
and they are fishing in the old creek, grandpa
loved to go to. What do you do if you catch a
fish? do you keep it? do you kill it and eat it? will
you eventually go to the bathroom and poop it
out? why are millions of people so afraid to ask
questions? you have the right to ask questions.
you have the right to demand answers. if the
answer you get then you are not happy then you
have the right to choose another option. Does
Jesus do this with all the other millions of
grandpas that have died? The first book I wrote I
was telling this story to some kids and a young
boy afterwards was learning in school that boys
are different then girls and that is an area no one
is supposed to touch or look at and if someone
does let a teacher or parent know about this, so
He asked me If God has legs, eyes, ears, mouth,
arms and body does God have a Penis? This was
the title of my first book published at Trafford
publishing. I was the crazy rebel preacher the
book was white with red letters showing the blood
of Jesus and every word was capital letters to
show I am a human being that does make
mistakes. then my second book Heaven right now
was all about Re-Incarnation and the third book
was titled Harmony, the Greatest story Never
Told all had capital letters then I changed to
create space, which is now kindle direct
publishing, and Amazon, so the rest of my books
all teach the same 5 truths just in various stories.
We know God did look down and see all the evil

going on and decided to destroy this world by a
flood, we know God has ears and hears our
prayers. We know God has a mouth and talks to
us, maybe not in a loud voice but sometimes we
feel the presence. does this God have a wife?
Yes, we call her Shekinah, the Queen of Heaven,
the Goddess, they both together created many
children, you call them angels, yes, a third of
these angels. led by Lucifer, the 1st born son had
a rebellion and were cast out of Heaven and now
are called rebel angels or demons. So, are their
good and evil out there today? Of course. which
one do you follow? The one you feed the most.
Feed evil and you become evil. Feed good and
you become good. You do have a choice. Why do
I say the same things over and over again? that is
how you remember, thru repetition, same as
taking a test, life is a test. No, you cannot change
the past. You can wake up and realize what you
have done and make changes Now. That is up to
you." End of chapter six scene six

Running thru the woods

Running thru the woods, as fast as I can,
am I a animal or am I a man?
chasing my lover, thru the woods I go,
I feel the tree limbs and the grass below,
the moon is bright and full tonight,
as we feel the wind and I keep her in sight.
suddenly she changes and flies away,
I look up and wonder, with nothing to say.
I wished real hard, with all of my might
and I sprouted wings and flew thru the night.
I shapeshifted to a raven, a surprise to me,
of all the different birds I wanted to be.
then she landed and changed to a wolf it seems
and I changed to, or is this only a dream?
The smell of grass, the wind in my face,
where did she go, gone without a trace,
I look and look, and cry out her name,
is this reality or is this only a game?
Then running thru the woods, as fast as I can,
am I really an animal or just a mere man?
copyright 2006 www.poetry.com   Melvin

Abercrombie

act 7 scene7 episode 7

now the sexy female voice talks again, " He knows he has to get ready to go to the big seminar, yes they will be waiting for me, his wife wants to go this time so they climb in back of their beautiful antique 1949 Rolls Royse, Brigitte and the film crew are always following in the company van, as his driver and body guard Jasmine escorts them, bill, the camera guy shows them leaving the estate, guards outside the gates wave as they pass and they head to the meeting place", Camera zooms in on cowboy Rex as he drives and talks "Yes, we are driving to Las Vegas, it is a very large auditorium, another state, another city.it is filled to capacity, everyone wanted to hear the crazy rebel preacher talk about being a immortal spirit/soul and named Merlyne and his new church, Avalon the Fishermen church ministry, most religions now do not worship a God and Goddess as equal no more, this we know for the last two thousand years religions have been divided, created their own form of Rebellion, scattered and confused to say the least. actually, we are just going back to the beginning to the first Olde Religion." The camera scans the audience, they are talking among themselves waiting on the one dog and pony show to start. Brigitte sets on the first row as half the crowd look at her and her resemblance to Marilyn Monroe, lots of heads turn and a lot of talking, the old couple walks out on the stage, smiling his wife sets down between the two guards, everyone is amazed they are used to seeing pictures of a old gray haired man but now this is obvious the same man but now bald headed and looking much younger, He walks up to the micro phone, takes it off the podium and reaches his hand out and a chair slides over to him. no one else see's this, not even the camera crew all they see is a old man, who now looks much younger, surprised he shaved his gray Hair all off looks funny as a bald man sort of like a Mr.

clean with his gray eyebrows and gray handle bar
moustache. Who was talking to himself, They
Laugh among themselves even Brigitte said he
looks much younger and sexy they were told to
follow the old man and record everything, this is
what they were paid to do. The old man was very
rich, Thru the years, he has been fair to people,
and they have made him rich beyond his means.
He wanted to share some of his motivational
stories, that is why Brigitte, and the film crew are
here.to follow him around, film his seminars and
go back to his mansion and listen to all the stories
of elusive treasures he is saying. yes, there is
another camera crew from the local Tv station,
they to want to record his talk and a lot of
preachers from local churches are here listening
to what he has to say. The old man holds his
hand up for people to listen and they do, He talks:
" I am Melvin Abercrombie, this lecture is all
about what if? What if there is a thing called re-
incarnation? What if you get the chance to go into
another life again and again? what if one life you
get to be rich, while another life you get to be
poor? What if I tell you I am a warlock or what
you would call a male witch? Do you believe me?
What if I tell you I am a real vampire who has
lived many lifetimes and I wrote over 50 books all
saying about the same thing, maybe a few
different stories but most are the same? Why? I
do not just believe in a female goddess, as most
wicca still do, I believe in equality yes, a male
God and a male son of this God you Christians
call Jesus Christ, the real messiah. What if I tell
you the real Jesus Christ never worshipped on
Sunday, the first day of the week? He kept the
true 7th day Saturday sabbath. you cannot show
me in any version of any holy bible anywhere
were Jesus worshipped on Sunday, the 1st day of
the week, you cannot because he never did, why
do you? most were told we are not under the old
law anymore, we can do whatever we want to do,
we are saved by grace, are you? What if I tell
you the real Jesus taught you that you do not just
get one chance at this game you call life and die

and go to a heaven forever and ever Jesus taught
re-incarnation. I teach and believe in re
Incarnation? What if I have lived many lifetimes
and so have you. I am a Warlock, yes, a real
vampyre and a rebel preacher which means to
me, I have not done anything so bad as God or
Goddess want to label me as a demon or bad
guy, but I realize the religions and church's today
are all wrong, so as a rebel I can slowly help and
show the world what they are doing wrong. Did
the Greeks? the Egyptians? Celtic and Teutonic
teach re-Incarnation? Can you experience all the
things you would like to experience in only one
lifetime? No way lots of different cultures did
believe in an afterlife whether this is Valhalla,
Heaven, Avalon or paradise some were taught
that only the kings and big leaders got to go and
do something, the common men or woman just
died and if they were good get to go to a heaven
forever and ever or if they were bad got to go to a
hell for ever and ever that was how a few in
charge could control the mass of people, the
scare technique. for those who do not know me,
yes, I have been searching for God all my life. I
have gone to various churches and different
religions trying to find out whose God is better
than the other God. I have studied most of the
rebellion type religions, Buddha, Hindu, Islam,
Jewish, 100 different Christianity, read the
different versions of the Holy Bible, studied
Wicca, Yes we will still have all our tenets of faith,
Christians, Jewish, Islam, Hindu, Buddha, etc. but
for those who are ready to simply go back to
when we had one Religion, I believe in the
beginning, long before Christianity, Islam, Jewish,
Buddha and Hindu Religions, then Adam and Eve
had one Religion. remember there were no other
religions only Adam, eve and their children. they
had one language, one religion, one church, one
male God and one female Goddess, we know
they had a lot of children, and we know there was
a rebellion long before all this were a third of
these children did get into a rebellion and were
cast out of heaven. Is this why God and Goddess

created mortal humans, Adam and Eve to give
their rebellious children something to rule over?
We know in the beginning the chosen people
where the Hebrew people, so did they speak the
Hebrew language? They were not originally
Circumcised, that was done much later by Moses
because of the desert and lack of water, we know
the family of Adam and eve did worship a male
God and a female Goddess all the way up to the
time Jesus Christ was alive and walking around.
We know the original Romans, who nailed him to
a cross, did worship a male God they called
Jupiter and a female Goddess as equal called
Juno. We know we can go to Rome Italy today
and still see the remnants of the God and
Goddess, Juno, we just call that the Olde
Religion, but it was the Religion that Jesus Christ
was aware of and He never told you otherwise.
Same as the Greeks, Zeus and Hera, Egyptians
Osiris and Isis you can still go there today and
see the temples and remnants, what happened?
Did they all die? Is the God of this world now
Lucifer? the original first-born son (Sun) of our
God and Goddess? Is he ruling the World today?
If our God and Goddess did die, then when will
they come back? Are we ready for them to come
back? That is what I am searching for. Can we
get a big giant pot and mix all the different
religions in it and stir them all up and pour out
one Religion? The way it was before all this
"scattered & confused?"   End of chapter 7

Leather and Blue Jeans

The wind in your hair, the sun on your face,
leather and blue jeans against satin and lace,
on back of a Harley, she would ride,
soulmate, lover, always at his side,
or is she a dream? for in reality,
could this be what we searched, thru all eternity,
for if this is a dream, I don't want to wake,
I want to stay forever, or for goodness sake,
for two hearts together, can become one,
every morning we arise, for our work is not done,
If life is so simple, when we are apart,

imagine together and feeling your heart,
for together anything is possible to do,
we can build that castle and paint it blue,
or white or green, it doesn't matter to me,
as long as your happy, for don't you see,
so now this poem must come to an end,
we are off on the Harley, going around the bend,
the wind in your hair, the sun on your face,
Leather and blue jeans against satin and lace.
copyright 2006 www.poetry.com by Melvin
Abercrombie

scene 8 act 8 episode 8

The scene can be another lecture seminar a large
church or auditorium, the old man has his old
black cowboy hat on for good luck," he paused
took a drink of coffee, then continued "we were
taught as a Christian that you only get one
chance at this game we call life, we experience a
few things then we die and get to go to a heaven
or burn in a hell for ever and ever is that it? One
of my other books I titled Xperience, great book
with a lot of the same stories to make a book with
so many words Now what if you were born in
Japan? you grew up being taught their culture,
their civilization, their language and their religion,
it's not your fault, you were taught that your God
is a big, fat, bald headed oriental guy named
buddha. Who is right? who is wrong? who gets to
decide? They believe in re-incarnation. I grew up
as a Christian Baptist and we were taught we are
not under that old law no more we are under
Paul's teaching which said we can eat whatever
we want to eat. Actually, Paul saw an Angel and
this Angel which told him, now its ok to eat
whatever you want to eat. that Angel was Lucifer,
the 1st born son of God who was cast out of
Heaven along with a third of the other Angels". " I
pause and look down the aisle of the giant
auditorium the back door opens and in walks
Lucifer, the first-born son, the true Rebel Angel
now called a Demon. He turns and waves his
hands and all the doors thru out the building
locked letting everyone know they are stuck here.

Rex and Jasmine draw their weapons and surround the old couple to protect them but protect them from what? Brigitte, the film crew and all the audience turns and looks like Lucifer walks down the aisle toward us. As he walks he shapeshifts into various beautiful male entities famous people like Elvis Presley, Rock Hudson, Tony Curtis, different woman and man will see what they want to see as he walks down the Aisle, then suddenly He shape-shifts into a hideous beast with horns and long demonic wings and flies around the building showing his power and flies down to the stage, the camera crew are all trying to film all this as he moves around and stands in front of me and his wings disappear and he shape shifts into a beautiful blonde hunk of a man he calls himself Georgio, smiling, he tells Rex and Jasmine that he is not going to hurt the old couple, they step back taking his wife with them, bewildered at what they saw, he grabs my microphone and the audience listens "What he says is true' Looking at me I fall on my knees, knowing the power He has and I curl up in a fetal ball, He continues: " I am the First born son, yes the first Rebel Angel, born long before my younger brother, your Jesus was born, created long before your Adam and Eve were born, some want to call me the devil or Satan or Lucifer and for thousands of years I tolerated your stupidity, Now I am Georgio, your God of this World, Yes our father and mother did die, that is why you see the time change from what you call bc to ad and i allowed you to think it was all about Jesus my little brother. I allowed him to live because it was our fathers dying wish and you think he died on a cross was more of this illusion. My brother Jesus was married, had lots of children just like me and he lived a long mortal life along with his wife, you call Mary Magdalene and along with his mother, you call the virgin Mary they did leave and traveled around the world, and all lived a good long life under my protection. I rule the sun and I am the God of this world. I am the one who divided you up thru out the years and you are

scattered and confused because I allow you to be
scattered and confused because of your stupidity.
I allowed the Olde world order to end and gave
stupid pathetic people millions of dollars to carry
out my New World order yes, we will go back to
one God, Me, one language the English language
and there will be one color of people and one
church one religion because I said so. Now I
realized father and mother created you for a
reason so now It is time for mother and father to
return and I will allow this, they have been waiting
on you mortal humans to wake up and realize you
need them both, but you have not heard the
calling. I will allow this man" He stops and turns
and points his finger down at me, and he grabs
my arm and smiling he pulls me back up "This
man, Melvin Abercrombie, who now ask the What
if Question, who now says he is a true Warlock
and a true Vampyre, yes, I agree I can read his
mind and know his heart is real. I allow this man
to teach you and He has my blessings to teach
the truth. He wrote these books to help teach you
these truths and these other secrets my brother
Jesus Christ was teaching, Yes God is my Father
and so the Man you call Jesus is my Blood
brother, we have the same father so do you, if
you open your pathetic eyes and realize when
you pray, you pray to our Father, Yahweh, No
one prays to Mother Shekinah anymore, they
want to call her a vampire Goddess, She is our
Mother, the Queen of heaven, the creator of all
but if they do, they want her to be a dominant
controlling creator, there is still no equality in
Wicca you are divided because I allowed you to
be divided, hoping you would wake up and realize
your pathetic wrong doings. I gave you chance
after chance after chance to wake up and see the
wrong. I sent preachers and teachers to help
persuade you, but you burned them or killed them
because you did not want to handle the truth. And
no one gives me the respect I deserve," Laughing
he says "Kind of like your comedian Rodney
Dangerfield, He gets no respect either" Laughs
again " and this is about the kosher food laws,

Father tried to teach you but you are so pathetic and easy to manipulate and You were taught you are a mortal, Temporary, flesh and blood Human but inside you there is an Immortal Spirit/Soul, so each life you are judged and you get to go into a new Re-Incarnated body according to my Father and Mothers will. So now this man", He pauses and puts his arm around me, smiling he says " Now has my blessings, listen to what he is saying, Read His books and learn the Truths, the secrets, it is time. Not much will change. I am still in charge, this is still my world, the time that changed from what you call B.C. to your A.D. I created. yes, another rebellion, my forces have grown, and we have overpowered our Father and Mother and now this is my world. I have started this New World Order. One male God, Me" Laughing pounding His chest "Father tried to create my brother Jesus to help as a last-ditch effort but I made sure he was killed to silence Him. I now have three times the power then they do so I allow certain things to happen if It pleases me, you have been given the opportunity to wake up and see who I really am. Yes Father and Mother are both watching you and you do have a choice, They are both standing by to see if I allowed this pathetic Christian religion to grow and gave them permission to think they are now worshipping a male God, actually me and I allow my brother Jesus to be there so they will accept it and i left the third entity as a Holy Spirit as my Father and Mother as Advisers to be the watchers. This is my world, I am Lucifer, now known as Georgio, the true first-born son and the rightful heir to the throne. I gave you a stupid thing to search for a simple Holy Grail and it took you thousands of years to figure it out the Holy Grail is the female side of all creation, Yes my Mother Shekinah, my sisters Auriel, who you call Mother Earth, my other sister Gabriel, who rules over the water and Eve and all the females in this creation process, the Holy Grail is the one church I would respect and that is Avalon Fishermen ministry, and a time will come, this man will help open the doors", He holds his hands up and thunder and lightning sounds all over the Auditorium, He waves his hands and wind and rain appears getting everyone soaking wet, thousands of people terrified out of their wits not able to leave, listening to the one Power strong enough to take over the Universe. I will allow mother and father to one day return, they give me their blessings and stand back and watch to see what you mortal humans will do, there is no such thing as time in our world, this is something you created, there is no past, no future only the now. Either you will keep going and eventually destroy yourself or you will wake up and read these books and understand the truths. " He turns, looks at the front row as his eyes meet Brigitte, smiling he says," is your grandmother, the fictional Marilyn Monroe? yes she replies he said "you want to go with me? smiling she says "hell yes" Lucifer turns and says "I will not hurt her, and I will bring her back to your mansion". Brigitte looks at Bill and Veronica and says "hope you are filming all this? Yes" they replied "good "she said, "I will be back later, send all the film like we do every day, do not worry about me" and they both walk out the door and all the doors are unlocked. The camera goes outside and see lucifer and Brigitte ride off in his beautiful shiny, old red Cadillac convertible with the longhorns bolted to his hood, now back inside, the audience goes crazy at what they just saw, me trembling and knees shaking set down for a moment. I look at the audience wondering what I need to do next, I stand up and grab the microphone and say, "Ok wow I need to continue my lecture did the other church camera crew film all this?" they nod their head, and he continues:" the movie producers can add all kinds of wild sex scenes were lucifer and the granddaughter of the fictional Marilyn Monroe at their discretion. now he speaks:" I do believe in Re-incarnation and have written several stories of me in one of my past lives.one time long ago during the black plague, my wife and children did die, why was I spared? I was a real Vampyre, no not the fake crap that Hollywood wants you to see, no, i do not drink blood or turn into a bat or a wolf, no i am not afraid of a cross or the sun I had powers back then did that save me? My suffering I went to the alcohol to calm down the demons inside of me, so the bottle of rum was my solace. One night at the local tavern a stranger bought me several rounds, Not knowing he was a part of a Pirate ship that needed deck hands to run the ship, drunk I was carried on the ship and next morning I awoke with a hangover far from land. I had two choices, work the ship or jump overboard and let the sharks eat me, not much of a choice, I figured as soon as I get close enough to see land maybe I could jump overboard and hope to make it but that never happened. One night I awoke to a lot of noise and explosions as I realized we were being attacked by another ship. I went on top deck to see a lot of people laying there dead. A man from the other ship came running at me with a sword and I knew I was about to die, I looked down and saw a sword next to a dead man and grabbed it to defend myself, I had two choices, die or kill this man. As He lunged at me, I stabbed him. I looked around and there was no one else close by so I grabbed His clothes and Money bag, his sword and threw his body overboard, I crossed the line from being a Rebel Angel to being a Demon, I broke Gods Law one of the Commandments, thou shalt not kill, so I knew I crossed the line and the Demonic spirit consumed me. He would have done the same to me. Killing got easier, each time I grabbed what money, coins, precious stones they carried and hid them thinking I will need something when I escape. then one night another Explosion, this time I knew the ship was sinking as I went on top deck I realized both ships were sinking, the captain and a few of his man were taking the lifeboats for them-selves so i grabbed a large door that was blown off hoping it would float I threw it over-board and with my money bag and all my possessions I too jumped overboard and

swam to the floating door. I tried to paddle away
and get far away from them as Possible. I woke
up the next morning looking at nothing, no ships,
no bodies, no anything. I cried out to the God and
Goddess to forgive me, yes, I deserve this, I killed
a man, but to me it was self-defense. I felt there
was a difference in killing in self-defense and pre-
meditated murder for the fun of it. I floated for
three days and three nights, Laughing, I realized I
was surrounded by all this food and starving to
death, surrounded by all this water and dying of
thirst. I tried drinking the salt water, but it made
me sick. Weak I realized I should die so I prayed
that this will be over with soon. I rolled off the
board, too weak to climb back on I accepted my
fate, then a Blonde hair woman came up behind
me and kept me alive, swimming in the dark for
what seemed an eternity then suddenly I felt the
sand beneath my feet, I struggled to get ashore,
turning around to think this beautiful blonde hair
woman I realized she was a mermaid, she
represented Gabriel, the Angel ruling the water
and direction of west and she swam off. I made it
ashore and dedicated the rest of that life to
teaching about God and the Goddess as Equal. If
you ask me, I will show you the two tattoos on my
left arm showing Gabriel as a mermaid and the
pirate ship I was on. you say, well this should be
in the last chapter about Re-Incarnation, but you
will see I am only a mortal Human who does
make mistakes and yes, we need to talk about
the kosher foods but the church itself allowed you
to eat pork and scavenger food because Paul
said it is Now ok, we are not under that Olde Law
but are we? We know the Roman Catholic church
did teach this Equality a Male God and a Female
Goddess now as the Virgin Mary. One way or
another the Roman Catholic religion did grow.
Those who did not approve protested and were
called the rebels or Protestant so did they rebell
or protest? to be nice we say they only protested,
which eventually evolved into the Baptist,
Methodist, Pentecostal, Church of God,
Presbyterian, Church of Christ and another 100

offspring Rebellion religions who now use the 3-pointed Triangle as their symbol and call their new religion a Trinity composed of a male God, Yahweh or Jehovah. The new first-born Son of God as Jesus Christ and another Male entity no one knows who he is as the Holy Spirit. So now we have gone from a world worshipping 7 Gods down to 6 Gods then wicca as 5 Gods and this new Religion as 3 Gods so who is right? Who is wrong? who gets to decide? It's only one God and one Goddess, we argue over which of these children do we recognize as important. If you fast forward to the last two thousand years to today and realize all the different religions, different denominations with different doctrines with different number of Gods and Goddess so who is right? The 7 Gods? the 6 Gods? the 5 Gods or the new 3 God Trinity? If we take the olde 7 Gods and add the teachings of Jesus Christ then we would have 8 Gods so is that worse? can we use the symbol of a Cross as four and another cross, maybe inverted equally and have a 8 pointed star? If we take the Teachings of Wicca with the 5-pointed star and add the Christian trinity teachings of 3 Gods, do we not have the same 8? Several people are trying to join wicca and Christianity together as the pure religion, they call it Christian Wicca and several books are out, is this so bad? This would be one step in the right direction, the problem would be there are so many different Christian Religions and a few different Wicca religions so to me letting everyone know that I am a Warlock, or a Male Witch would let people see what the Olde Religion is really all about. Long ago there was no separation there was no male God Religions and no female goddess religions there was no separation only one Church, One Religion we Honor the Male God, the female Goddess and we call upon the guardians of the Directions North as Auriel, East as Raphael, south fire as Michael and west water as Gabriel we changed to going East first because Lucifer is the Sun God and he wanted the east, Raphael as his male brother to go first making North, Auriel as Mother earth as last to show his superiority so again, who is right? who is wrong? who gets to decide? Now what would the One Church that Adam and Eve would go to Be Called? They worshipped the 7 Gods, there were no Catholic, Baptist, Methodist, Church of God etc. there were no Jewish, Islam, Buddha, Hindu or other rebel religions. If we add the Teachings of Jesus Christ then yes, we will now have 8 Gods or only One God and one Goddess as Equal and the Teachings of their children, the Angels and Demons. Could we add the Teachings of the Hindu? Buddha? Islam? and other Religions? are they to a form of Rebellion? We want to think when we die and get to go to Heaven forever there will be one God, one Church one Religion, for ever and ever, so what is that Church? Do we have to wait till we die to see that Church? Can we have our cake and eat it too now? I want to Think of Avalon   the Church Ministry. If you stop and think about the name then, yes Avalon was the female side of the equation and Anglesey was the male side, this was part of the division, we have no power if we are divided. We are all mortal, flesh and blood temporary humans. Yes, every one of you are a mortal, temporary, flesh and blood human" as he points his finger in different directions so the camera could see he is showing everyone. "You also are an immortal spirit soul, yes, you have lived many lifetimes. You cannot possibly experience all the things you need to experience in only one lifetime." He pauses for that to sink in looks around drinks another sip of coffee then continues "You cannot experience all the things you need to experience in a hundred lifetimes, it's not your fault, all you know is what you were taught. All they can teach you is what they were taught. I will say this over and over. You cannot be born a male and a female, and be able to create children, you cannot be black, white, oriental, Spanish, in only one lifetime. You cannot be a doctor ,lawyer, artist, electrician, plumber, architect, engineer etc. all in one lifetime, So God allowed you to experience the things you need to experience during this lifetime, We are all here to experience different things, and we will talk more into this later, but for now understand, You are a immortal spirit soul, trapped in a mortal flesh and blood temporary body to experience the things you need to experience during this lifetime. When you die, your mortal, flesh and blood, temporary body dies. You came from a female, and you will return to a female, you have this male trinity of our God, the Father, Yahweh, and now thru Christianity you have this new son of God who you call Jesus Christ, yes, He is the Ha Mashiach, the Yeshua Christus, but then you have another entity you call a male Holy Spirit? So, who could this other male be? There is only one other male and that is the real, Rebel Angel who became a Demon, first born son of God, Lucifer, the Greeks called Hades, the God of the Underworld. but wait you say, he is Satan, he is the Devil, we were taught to curse Him, to hate him, to bind him, yes, I grew up as a Christian Baptist, If you go back to before Jesus was born and the New Testament was written, long before Moses was born and the old Testament was written, long before Adam and Eve and this World was created Our Male God and Our Female Goddess, together did Create many Children." I pause Look around wanting that to sink in, take another drink of coffee I hold my hand up to show my cup is empty and everyone in the audience freezes, amazed I look around only the ghost camera is recording everything, yes all the camera crew and everyone is frozen in time, smiling I walk over to the coffee pot, pour another cup of coffee, walk back to the podium and raise my hand again as everything goes back to normal, I continue " Yes God and Goddess did create many children, you call them Arch Angels, The first born Son is called Lucifer, You all just seen him or her in all their Glory. we all know the story of how he, and a third of His Brothers and sisters did Rebell and were cast out of Heaven and we will talk more about that later, even when

Jesus Christ was alive many cultures did worship a male God and a female Goddess as equal, The Romans, Jupiter and Juno. The Greeks, Zeus and Hera, The Egyptians, Osiris and Isis, The Celtic, Cerrunos and Cerridwen and Teutonic, with Odin and Freya. So, we only had this male trinity for less than two thousand years. What about the female side? Could they too have a female trinity? If we think of the Goddess as the other side of God as one, then the first-born daughter, Auriel, we call Mother Earth and Gabriel as ruler of water or some want to add Eve, the first-born female in all this flesh and blood mortal, temporary human body. Ok you say but what about Adam? are we forgetting Adam? If you read the Bible, Jesus taught Reincarnation, again you cannot experience everything in only one lifetime so to me the bible teaches that Jesus Christ is the word and the word was with God from the Beginning so Now that shows me that Jesus, flesh and blood, mortal, temporary human is a Re-Incarnation of Adam I realize I am saying a whole lot in a short period of time and yes, This does overwhelm you, Yes It overwhelms me, I asked God to give me this understanding heart and the out pour came so fast yes it is overwhelming so I will repeat a lot of this over and over. End of Chapter eight act 8 scene 8

The Flood

The year I don't remember, right before the flood, Noah called the animals, the way God said he should,　　　　I remember thunder, lightning, people crying below,　　　　to late for God's forgiveness, you reap what you sow,　　　　for 40 days and nights, the rain came pounding down,　　　　no one, not even the animals were making a sound,　　　　a new world we created, under God's Law from above,　　　　no murder, stealing, hating, we had only love.
Then thru the years, the devil, for he survived it seems　　　and the evil we tried to lose, was only just a dream.　　　　The year I don't remember, it was right before the flood,　　　My Father

called the animals, the way God said He should
copyright 2006 www.poetry.com by Melvin
Abercrombie

scene 9 act 9 episode 9

The old man was again talking " there was a story
about two brothers, we could change the story
around and say there were two sisters a little
rebellion? Yes, one was a good, Christian, went
to church every time the doors were open, gave
his ten percent, became a good deacon, then
later an elder and eventually died, he went to
heaven, stood before God, no problem, went thru
the pearly gates, down the streets of gold and sat
in his mansion, looking down he saw his evil
brother, who killed, stole, broke every law, was
dying in a hospital, he asked the doctor to send a
preacher, the doctor called his Pentecostal
preacher to drop by, the evil brother said I have
done a lot of bad things, can you pray for me?
Yes, Halleluiah, Praise the Lord you are saved
by Grace, all you have to do is say the three
magic words and you get to go to heaven forever
and ever, if you do not, you will burn in a fiery hell
forever and ever, the brother, reached out to his
drawer, pulled out his billfold in the drawer and
said here is three hundred dollars, all that I have
tell me what are the 3 magic words?, the
Preacher took the money put it in his pocket and
said halleluiah, praise the lord, all you have to do
is say "God forgive me" and really mean it over
and over, the sick brother cried out "Please God
Forgive me, please God forgive me, then He
died, He went to heaven, God said well done my
son, He too walked thru the pearly gates, down
the streets of gold and into a mansion, right next
door to his brother, who cried out, "God, Father,
that is not fair, I went to church every Sunday,"
God Replied, "Nowhere in any part of my Holy
Bible did I ever command you to go to any church
on Sunday, the 1st day of the week, I always told
you to keep my 7th day Saturday Sabbath, well,
the brother cried out, I gave that preacher ten
percent of my money every week, he told me he

was going to put in a good word for me." God replied "Where is that preacher at now? He spent your money buying that mansion, pretty cars, airplanes, and saying he should all be tax exempt, Joseph and Mary were heading to Bethlehem to pay their share of taxes, Jesus always paid his share of taxes, no church or religion should declare themselves tax exempt, so now you see what is wrong with all these thousands of different religions, I created Avalon as a non-denominational church that accepts every one, no matter what Religion they were born in. All you know is what you were taught. Your sub-conscious will only accept what you tell it to believe in and they only know what they were taught, yes, I will say that over and over only thru repeated words will you remember things. Would it be so bad to have one big Religion were everyone agrees? Yes, there is a Male God, now whatever name you want to call this God is up to You. We all speak a different language, so we have different belief's but it's still the same Male God, Whatever name you want to call Him. The same with the female side of God, she has many names, its ok to be Involved in immortality cowboy church and still call her by whatever name makes you happy, If you say a prayer then you are calling upon that God or Goddess, so call all of the Religions are one, it's the same. Another group calls them-selves Christian Wicca, they do mean well, she is trying to join the 5 gods, Female Goddess Wicca Religion with the 3 Gods Christian Religion which is Great. Which Christian religion goes with Wicca? Baptist? Methodist? Catholic? Protestant? Now what about all the Other Religions? What about Islam? Do you create Islam Wicca? or Jewish Wicca or Hindu Wicca? See my point only when we combine all the Religions and call upon our God and our Goddess thru prayer will they hear us. In Wicca they go thru three Initiations, I know I studied them myself, yes they have a High Priestess who oversaw everything and you cast your circle of protection and call upon the four children of the

Goddess for protection from the demonic forces out there, back then it was with the opening to the East because the Sun did rise from the east and that was the way we were taught. , To me, that does not make sense, the guardian of the east is Raphael, He is the air, Do we honor him first? I always thought the opening should be from the north, that way Auriel, our Mother Earth, would get the respect first, of course you would enter the circle, call upon your Goddess first, but why can't we call upon our God, Yahweh also? then we face North and call upon the guardian of the north, which was at the beginning, she was the first-born daughter. If You go back in time before Adam and Eve then we know there was a male God, I call Him Yahweh and he did have a wife, I call her Shekinah, for over 2,000 years society and churches have hidden Her. I was taught that the chosen people were the Hebrew people so to me, I would choose the Hebrew name of our God and Goddess. They had children you call them Angels or Arch Angels. The first-born Son was called Lucifer and the first-born daughter was Auriel. We know there was a rebellion and a third of the Arch Angels, led by Lucifer were cast out of Heaven. Where did these fallen angels go? Where are they now? What if the demons are among us now? Of course, Lucifer was cast to the Sun, He Is the first born and he Is the Light. Auriel did not take a part of this Rebellion; she was given this earth and we call Her Mother Earth. God and the Goddess created mortal humans to give Lucifer and the fallen Angels something to rule over. God stood back and watched to see what they would do, after a while God said He wished He would have never created Mankind, why? He saw all the evil that Lucifer and the Fallen Angels created, and He tried to destroy it with a flood. These are things you already know.   Now when we combine the 3 Initiations of Wicca to the male creator Religions what will happen? Just like any military service, be it Army, Navy, Marines, air Force or? we know there are Privates, Sergeants

and Officers so as you go thru your 3 initiations
you can become a member of Avalon church
Ministry, it takes many many Privates to run any
church, and this is no exception. as you go thru
your second Initiation you become more of a
Sergeant or a Deacon of the Church with more
responsibility and if you want to go thru the 3rd
initiation and Become an Office or Elder of the
Church and some become Preachers themselves and branch out and build other Avalon
Fishermen church ministries. Would the World be
a better place if we had an Avalon Fishermen
church Ministry in every city, every state all over
the World? I like to see a male high priest and a
female high priestess as the elders or officers.
They can be husband and wife or what the
Church chooses each Avalon Ministry will have
as its members a lot of different people with
different religious backgrounds, we will have to be
called Rebel Angels because we are rebelling
against the religious system so can you handle
that? the common thread is the willingness to
agree upon an equal male creator God and a
female creator Goddess, there will be general
congregational members and those who want to
go thru the 3 initiations as members, Deacons
and Elders to help run the Church in its daily
activities. I choose Yahweh as the male creator's
name and Shekinah as my female Goddess
creator name, why? Once again, I believe the
chosen people were called the Hebrew people,
this is not the Circumcised Jewish people, The
original Hebrew were Not Circumcised. Adam
and all of his sons were not Circumcised and all
the way down to Noah and His Sons, Shem, Ham
and Japheth were Not Circumcised. This was a
clean Issue brought out by Moses much later,
due to being in a desert and lake of water to
cleanse yourself so it was a clean issue., It does
not matter now if you are Circumcised or not that
is not the problem. Even Jesus was allowed to be
butchered as a Jewish person. Now I did go thru
the 3 Initiations of Wicca. Originally a long time
ago they recommend going thru each initiation as

a year and a day but now we realize so many people are faster while others are slower so there is no time limit. Each Wicca is different I had to go before the Group who formed a big circle and stand in the middle so all could see me. They asked me questions about what i believed in and asked me did I know the Wicca rede? This is the first eight words you have to memorize by heart. The Christian motto was 11 words and its "Do unto others as you would have them do unto you" The Wicca rede is "And You Harm None Do What You Will" We are under that law meaning physically, mentally or spiritually and you harm none, do what you will is the Law. The Christian religion you have to accept Jesus as your lord and savior and be saved to be a member of the Christian Church. In Wicca you have to accept the Goddess as the Creator of all. The people look at you and it's a majority to vote you in as a member. As Avalon Ministry we would add the male God, Yahweh as equal to the Goddess and accept both as equal as part of the 1st initiation and become a member of the church or a Private in Gods army and a true Rebel Angel, now being able to wear the Rebel Angel Patch on your jacket or coat so all the World will see who you are. The second initiation you are baptized a lot like Christians instead of putting you into a tank of water and dunk you under you are in a Shower to wash away your sins but you are told you are not saved by grace but accountable, you do not get to go out commit whatever sin you want to and right before you die get to say the 3 magic words God forgive me and get to go to a Heaven forever and ever, life does not work that way again before the baptism you are in the middle of the circle so everyone can see you and ask questions and now you must recite the whole wicca rede not just the 8 words. Do you know the whole wicca rede? If i remember right it goes something like this. "Obey the Wicca Law you must, In Perfect love, in perfect Trust. Eight words the rede fulfil, and you Harm None, do what You will, least of all in thy own presence it be, forever mind the rule of three, follow this in mind and heart, and merry you meet, and merry you part." As the church grows, we decide, do we want to change the wording from Wicca to Avalon. We do not want to call our self's wicca even though we accept a lot of the wicca teaching. We also accept the true teaching of the Rebel Angel, our Yeshua who you call Jesus Christ. something close to that, the members vote on you then you get to be baptized thru the shower washing away the unclean. Now you become a deacon or in the army of God and Goddess you are a sergeant The third initiation i went thru I had to cast my own circle, call upon our Mother Goddess as creator of all, face the east and call upon Raphael and ask for his protection, then go clock-wise, deosil, face south and call upon Michael the fire spirit and ask for his protection and then Gabriel the water spirit of the west and ask for her protection, last face north and call upon Her as Auriel, Mother earth and ask for her protection. Then once we are protected inside our circle we can do church business, pray for those needing help and just like any Christian Church ask the Gods for blessings if needed. then when all is done, we reverse the procedure or widdershin and go back and thank each Arch angels for their blessings Each time we stand and face the direction of the Guardians and pray to them and ending our circle with the Goddess. The only difference in Avalon would be we add the male God Yahweh and the female Goddess as Shekinah as Equal and ask for both of their protection as equal. We open the circle facing North and call upon the first-born daughter Auriel Mother Earth first then go clockwise or deosil to the east and Raphael. now we will call our Religion Avalon Ministry so I would Like to change the casting of a circle which is temporary and use a permanent full bubble circle completely surrounding you 24 hours a day 7 days a week 365 days a year. You have the guardian of the north in honor of Auriel, our mother earth, then go clockwise to Raphael the guardian of the east, deosil to south where

Michael is the guardian of the south and fire and then go to west, where the guardian is Gabriel, and she rules the water then on around back to the north to complete the circle. one difference is we do call upon our Goddess and our God to come into our circle of protection. Instead of just teaching that Auriel, Mother Earth just rules the north we believe Mother earth is everywhere, so is Raphael the Air spirit and Michael the fire spirit and Gabriel the water spirit, yes originally, they were assigned the guardians of different directions but it's important to show they are all over the World in every direction. Here we can add the rebel teachings of Christ and invite him into the circle, do we now have the 5 Gods of Wicca and the 3 Gods of Christianity so do we have 8 Gods now? No, we have two Gods or a Male God, Yahweh and His Wife, Shekinah as the Goddess as Equal. We accept the Teachings and ask for the Protection from the sons and daughters of this God and Goddess. What about gays and lesbians? God made it very clear this a abomination read the story about sodom and Gomorrah and the flood. they did not obey God and were all destroyed, we as Christians hate the Islam because they hate lesbians and gays but actually, they obey gods' laws. they also keep the kosher food laws and call us infidels because we think that now its ok to eat pork and other scavenger foods. we as Christians were taught now, we can worship a male dominant god on Sunday the 1st day of the week, but Avalon keeps the 7th day Saturday sabbath. So now it's up to You and the congregation. You keep going to your false church's and pray God will forgive you on judgement day or wake up and read the bible and obey the law. Jesus said in Matthew 5 that he did not come here to change the law not one tit or tittle and anyone who does is considered least in my kingdom, later they added he came to fulfil, God allowed his son to die to do away with the animal sacrificial law only. Why should an innocent animal die for something you did? So now instead of casting a temporary circle, go into the circle say your request then close the circle down. you keep the circle or bubble all over you to protect you from evil, believe me If Lucifer sees a chance to enter, He will., What do you want to learn? Are you happy with just only the teachings of Jesus? Would the world be a little better If you Incorporate some Buddha, Hindu, Jewish and Koran teachings to your congregation? Are you going to burn in hell forever If you decide to open your doors and let others teach you a little about their Religions? In the Old Wicca the Male was Her consort or during the spring festival He came, planted his seed, then lived thru the summer and fall, then died out during the winter, that was their way because they did not agree with all the different male dominant creator religions. Now the male God does not die out He Is equal to the Goddess, yes, He plants his seed and the Female in all creation do the creating together in balance, perfect love perfect trust so now as we go thru the third initiation, we become an Elder or a officer in the Army of God and Goddess. Do we just support one church or do we realize we need to branch out and as a new preacher can we build another Avalon Fishermen church Ministry in another area or town? ." He pauses takes a drink of coffee looks around then Continues " Now Avalon Worship's a Male God, Yahweh and a Female Goddess, Shekinah as Equal. We keep a lot of the teachings of Wicca, instead of casting a circle then go thru all the trouble to uncast we create a full 360-degree bubble of protection and ask the guardians for their protection and Christianity also Jewish, Hindu, Buddha and Islam even the Egyptian teachings. I did memorize the Wicca Rede or now do we want to say Avalon Law? I want to Incorporate it as part of our initiation keep the same first initiation as being saved, as a private and a member. the second as being baptized and a sergeant and a deacon and the third as making your own circle showing the congregation you have the knowledge to open a circle of protection and be a active officer or elder to help build up the congregation or help build more Avalon church ministries in other areas or towns. Something close to that. It needs to be a requirement for a person to go thru this understanding as part of our Avalon Church. We are just like any other church, you join and are told there are tenets they believe in, doctrinal Issues and being able to recite the basic rede or Avalon law of three. I am under the three-fold Law, If I do good then my God and Goddess may bless me, but If I do evil, I have seen up to a threefold curse. It is our law. Christians use the eleven words of their law to say the same thing "Do unto others as you would have then do unto you" it's the same as our law of eight words "And You Harm None, Do What You Will" are we under the 10 commandments? Yes, you cannot go out and kill people or steal things so yes, we are under God's Law, Jesus Christ Is still one of the sons and daughters of our God and Goddess and one of our teachers, he taught us "If you love me then keep my Commandments" What would it hurt if a Islam came to our church and studied the Christian and Guardian ways? What If he taught us some of the teachings of the Koran? Would we be more "Enlightened?" So is Islam, Buddha Hindu and the Jewish Rabbi's teaching different? It's the same God and the teachings are the same. I would Like different speakers from different denominations to join our Ministry and teach us the different what if teachings, not just Wicca, But Christian, Islam, the Koran, the Buddha, the Egyptian teachings, and the Hindu and the Lost books, Nag Hammadi, Dead Sea scrolls and forgotten books of the Bible, and others. There is so much we, as a church ministry, need to learn. I do have one rule, we will never pass the offering plate around. Yes, it does take a lot of money to make a Church Ministry work. Each Immortality cowboy church Ministry at the entrance door will have a big box bolted to the floor with a lock and a slot in top saying Tithes, Offerings and Prayer Request. Anyone who feels they want to be a part of the Ministry can put in their money; you will not be Judged if you do not give ten percent. This is something between you and God/Goddess. The more you give the more you get back, it's the Law, yes you want a fancy building. Then someone must pay for it. You want air condition, heat and lights? Then someone must Pay for it. You want music and people to work at the Church? Then they expect to get paid for their services, it would be nice If everyone did this for free, But reality is, if you want to be a part of any church ministry, It does take money. Can we do this and not call ourselves Rebel Angels? Can we walk around and not have this large Rebel Angel Patch on the back of our shirts, Jackets and other garments we wear to show others we are proud to be called the 1% or the Rebel Angels do others want to persecute us? do we hide our church because we are afraid of retaliation? Can we follow the other 99% of the people who think they are doing God's work? What gives us the right to say we are right, and they are wrong? Can Common sense prevail?" I hold my hand up to show my coffee cup is empty, short break, Then rest of the lecture:" End of chapter 9 act 9 scene 9

Fly Away

I can close my eyes, and I can fly away,
to another time, to another day
I dream of oceans, far and wide,
I dream of my lover, always by my side.
Arm in arm ******* hand in hand,
we feel the ocean, our toes touch the sand.
The moon is full and bright tonight,
as we gaze at the stars, above the firelight.
for a relationship to last and last,
they must think of the future, forget the past.
Let each other know, thru out the day,
sometimes it's just the little things that we say.
Next morning, we awake, sun shining bright,
we remember the little things of last night
The tender kisses, the walk on the sand,
the way we made love, the holding of hands.
for now, we must go back, a job we must do,

but I can think back and when I am feeling blue.
I can remember, another time, to another day,
I can close my eyes and I can fly away.
Copyright 2006 www.poetry.com   Melvin
Abercrombie

act 10 scene 10 episode 10

Brigitte and the film crew were allowed to stay as his guest for the next few days and his butler's and maids would provide for them. New act, new scene at the mansion, another lecture, camera crew filming everything, now with a new fresh cup of coffee the old man continues "I was taught from the day I was born that I was a Christian Baptist, and we are no longer under the law but saved by grace and now we can eat what other scavenger food we want to eat. My grandpa raised pigs and it was now ok to eat pork, catfish, lobster shrimp and other unclean foods. I remember my Grandpa who always told me "A man is only as good as his word, When you can look a man or woman In the eye, shake their hand and give your word then that is all you need" but now people lie to you, they steal and kill for money, no, money Is not the root of evil, It's how you obtain it. God even told you He does not want you to be poor. Grandpa was very religious, Dad was the opposite, yes, He was very wealthy and tried going to church, when I was a Child but the false preachers who kept saying give me ten percent of your money or you will burn in a hell forever pushed dad away. So, we quit going to Church. I looked for the real God in various churches and religions but finally gave up when mom died from cancer, she believed God could have healed her, but all our money could not. Cancer is an evil, deadly, necessary disease. I realize now, it's a bacteria, just like anything, you are what you eat, and Mom smoked and ate Scavenger food. Doctors tried to tell Her to stop smoking but she would not give It up, it was too late for Her so the last few years I realized Mom

had to experience dying with this disease we call
cancer, she needed to experience this for herself.
Sure, I can write a book telling you all about the
pain, suffering but until you actually experience
these things, walk a mile in their shoes, so now I
understand different people are here to
Experience different things, you see babies being
born with some disease and your heart goes out,
why? Could they have done some bad things in a
previous life? Instead of Just going to a heaven or
hell forever could God/Goddess allow that person
to go thru their version of their hell by being born
with a disease and going thru day in and day
out?" He pauses takes another drink , walks over
to the chalk board, picks up a piece of chalk and
as he talks he draws what he is trying to say, then
continues " I realize I said a lot of things I really
wanted to break all this down to only one topic at
a time, Spend one Seminar just talking about the
Female side of God and the original 5 star and 5
Gods of wicca and then add the 3 Trinity and the
3 male Gods of the Christian Religion not just
showing the 8 Gods now but showing we worship
a Male God and a Female Goddess as equal and
the teachings of their children known as Arch
Angels. Avalon Fishermen church Ministry is not
just joining the 5 Gods of Wicca along with the 3
Gods of Christianity we are creating a equality
religion that when you die and believe you get to
go to a heaven forever and ever then this would
be that religion, you do not have to wait till you
die, you get it now, for all those who are ready to
accept." Now rex talks" The seminar was great
the old man said the same things over and over
again the camera crew was told to film everything
no matter what, They could get all the film back at
the Hollywood gossip and go thru it, delete all the
scenes they wanted to and get this down to a one
or two hour movie, people would want to see.it
would make a great series, a little each week, like
the movie series Game of Thrones or
Yellowstone, so yes they were paid a great sum
of money to follow the old man around and now
he is going back to his mansion and tomorrow will

start a new elusive story type treasure He calls
them. The next scene is a typical school
classroom this can be a typical college type
seminar class-room with a lot of people there just
like any college class room" Melvin Abercrombie
speaks "If you look at all the different Church
Denominations out there and see most do this on
a Sunday, the 1st day of the week and now you
realize Jesus would never go to a church on a
Sunday, the 1st day of the week so now you
realize there is a lot of false teaching type
church's that really do mean well, they were just
taught wrong and now will not listen to common
Logic. this is Theology 101 teaching about our
Jesus Christ, the Rebel Angel, the Messiah or the
Ha Mashiach as he is called in the Jewish
language, yes, we did talk a little about the what if
in other chapters this is very important and only
thru repetition will we remember things,
remember in school to prepare for a test you had
to go over what was important to pass the test?
You are taking a test called life 101 you are
involved in this every day every week every
month and every year. The Jewish and other
religions do not think of our Jesus Christ as the
Messiah the True son of God. To them, yes, He
was a good man and did teach a lot of good
things but if you read the different Versions of the
Holy Bible and try to under-stand why they do not
believe this then you too may have doubt. We all
know that each book of the Holy Bible is just one
person's opinion of what they think actually did
happen, that is why it's called a "Version" If you
look at the first few books of the New Testament
then you will see Matthew, Mark, Luke and John
are all telling you Their Version of what they think
actually did happen and if you read all of these
four books you will see four different versions of
what did happen, Each one as a Human being
remembers different things. Now also remember
when each of these books were actually written.
Most were forty or more years later, why? The
early Leaders were scared of being prosecuted
and nailed to a cross like their Yeshua was, so

they had to hide for a while. Different people will tell you different dates of each book actually being written but it is believed the earliest book is Mark around 44 ad and the others Matthew, Luke and John were written around fifty or early sixty ad. The actual day they were written does not matter what does matter is they tried to write down what they believed actually did happen. Now also remember they did not have fancy Computers, telephones, Camera and typewriters to type in all this happening. They had animal skins, rocks and papyrus type paper to write on so this did not last very long and had to be re-written again and again thru the years The Good thing is all four books do have a lot in common, telling about the birth, life and all the good deeds He has done and the death and Crucifixion of our Lord and Savior and His coming back on the third day and eventually going up to a Heaven forever and ever. I like Luke's Version, Remember Luke was not a Jewish person, He was an Uncircumcised Gentile who was a Doctor and Follower of the Yeshua. Yes, Luke wanted to watch and follow this man who could heal Diseases how do you learn anything but by watching and seeing this with your own eyes? Luke also understood there were many Cultures and Languages going around at this time so many people could speak the Hebrew to be able to trade with them but also know the Roman Language because they were there. I believe Luke could speak several different languages as a doctor he had to understand this. to be able to treat People and be a doctor. Luke also understood that may cultures and Civilizations did have different Religions what was his Gentile Religious beliefs? Luke knew the Jewish called their male God Yahweh and their female Goddess was Shekinah, Queen of Heaven and the Romans called Their male God Jupiter, and their Goddess was Juno, did the Greeks hang around at this time? We do know that a lot of the original Hebrew language was translated into Greek and Latin but was this much later? We know the Greeks called their male God Zeus and their Goddess was Hera we already talked about that so what did the Gentiles believe in? What did they call their male God and Their female Goddess? We know that Luke believed the Spirit of God did go into the Virgin Mary, does not matter what male name you want to call this spirit of God, Yahweh, Jupiter, Zeus Odin or whatever. We know that Joseph was from the Tribe of Judah, why would God Pick someone from the rightful tribe of Judah with the right DNA to bring forth the Ha Mashiach then at the last moment not use him? This is why the Jewish people believe that Jesus could not be their messiah because he did not come from the right bloodline Luke was not there but was told the Spirit of this Male God did go into the Virgin Mary. Luke also understood that for Joseph and the Virgin Mary to be Legally married then they had to sleep together to consummate the wedding vows. Luke knew that a Angel came down and Told Joseph to not lay with the Virgin Mary so were they legally married? No according to the Jewish Laws of the day. Did God break his own laws of Deuteronomy 22? Did God Marry the virgin, Mary? No, she was already promised to Joseph. Did the Virgin Mary cry out? No so is she guilty of stoning according to Jewish laws at the Time for not saying anything? You decide. Now Luke also knows there is a female side of God we call the Goddess She is also known as the Holy Ghost, so Luke also says after the Spirit of God goes into the Virgin Mary, He puts the Word AND, and says the Holy Ghost went into the virgin Mary. Anytime you use the word AND then you are saying this happened AND this happened So Luke is telling us in His version And the Holy Ghost went into the virgin Mary to show us that God did not break His own laws of Deuteronomy 22 that His spirit and the Goddess spirit as Shekinah, Juno, Hera, Freya or whatever name you want to call this Goddess, She is the Holy Ghost that the Hebrew letters were finally translated into as the female side of God to create the baby Jesus. What if the spirit of God actually went into Joseph the rightful father AND the Holy Ghost, the Goddess spirit went into the virgin Mary and Joseph was told to have sex with His wife and God and Goddess in Spirit had sex and a child was Born the rightful Ha Mashiach the Tribe of Judah that only Joseph could provide. So, this would make our Jesus the Rightful Ha Mashiach, but the Jewish Rabbi knew they had to kill this man to silence him, so they changed what you were taught, and the early Christian's were also hunted, killed and had to flee for a while. I know you are thinking what proof do I have? Just common sense. The Jewish people today do not accept our Jesus as their Messiah, why? They too were taught the last two thousand years that Joseph did not have sex with His wife, so the marriage was not Legal, and this Jesus did not have the bloodline from Joseph who did have the right bloodline of the Tribe of Judah the Lion of Judah and their Ha Mashiach has to come from the bloodline of the tribe of Judah, they are still waiting on their Messiah. We also know that the virgin Mary was from the Tribe of Levi, the Priestly tribe, so yes, a child born with both of these bloodlines would give the right bloodline of the Ha Mashiach, but the Jewish Rabbi's had a scam going they were getting very wealthy by using the animal sacrificial Law by letting everyone just go out do whatever you want to do and bring an animal or money and they will atone for their sins and the Jewish Rabbis were getting away from this Goddess worship, they did not want any female to be a rabbi or equal with their male God, so they hid her from the religion, slowly a little at a time. When this Jesus Christ came along teaching this equality and putting down the animal sacrificial laws, they knew they had to kill him to silence Him, could they have found out that maybe Jesus was never circumcised? We know joseph and Mary were told to flee to Egypt, did a angel tell them to not butcher the Son of God or any more of their male children we know they had? Could this be why we do not really know about these lost years from the age of 13 to the last years? They made Jesus a Rabbi, did they later find out he was not circumcised, and they had to kill him to silence him? What gives anyone the right to change what our God created? Just because you are to lazy to pull the fore skin back and clean it, You are butchering an innocent baby created in the image of our God and changing him, what about all the millions, billions of males born before Moses started this mark of the beast by cutting the fore skin off of the head of the penis and permanently marking that male child for life , did our God circumcise Adam or any of the males born? No, was Noah or any of his male son's butchered or circumcised? Did any of the Romans, Greek or Egyptians circumcised? No, At the time my two sons were born I thought it was the right thing to do, so I allowed that to happen, knowing what I know now I would never allow that and I apologize to my son Kevin, My other son, Keith died, a father is not supposed to bury a son but I felt what God must have felt watching His son die." I stop the lecture to have a break for lunch. The camera hears a noise from the back door and zooms in to see what it is. Brigitte and the film crew turn and start filming and Rex, jasmine and my wife stand up to see what was going on and a woman, a very beautiful woman walks down the aisle towards the front, I turn to show rex, his wife and Jasmine that all is ok, no harm will be done, be still and watch. every one turn to see her as she too shape-shifts into different images, you call this trick camera or special effects, so it is up to the movie producer and directors to show a lot or a little. I look up from the lecture podium and smiling I open my arms to greet Her knowing this is the Arch Angel Gabriel, ruler of water and the direction of West. Before she gets to me, to show her power, a pair of Angel wings appear, and the back doors all lock so everyone knows they cannot run away, and she flies around and shapeshifts into various images to show yes, she is an Arch Angel ruler over water and a Child of our God and Goddess. I get on my knees with my hands up in the air and bow my head crying because I know the power she has. Am I teaching the wrong thing? Did She come here to kill me to silence me? It's easy to have a heart attack and suddenly die people do this all the time, head bowed, I waited for my fate, She Lands in front of me and grabs the microphone from the podium and talks to the congregation "Yes I am Gabriel The Guardian of water and I come here to listen to this man try to tell you the what if truths of what really did happen. I was there when my father, Yahweh and my mother Shekinah did help create this Yeshua Christus who you now call Jesus Christ, he is my little brother what this man, Melvin Abercrombie, is telling you is true" she stops, walks over to me and pulls me back up and gives me a big hug, thru tear-filled eyes trying to smile I stand up as she continues. " The world is ready for our mother to return. You have hidden her for too long, almost two thousand years now, yes, it is time for equality We are in the Age of Aquarius, and we need this Equality back if you, as mortal humans will ever survive, it is up to you. I approve of this Avalon Fishermen Church Ministry and see the reason of the Rebel Angels to do our will, they have my blessings and support, so now I will leave. You will go eat your lunch and come back and " listen to this man he has my blessings also Thank you" She put the microphone back on the podium and walked out. Brigitte looks at bill and veronica and says, "Wow, I hope you filmed all that," "yes" they replied, now we ate a good lunch and now back to the lecture. A lot of people raised their hands to ask questions I replied: "Yes as far as I can tell you got to meet the real Arch Angel Gabriel, was this all-movie hype? did the camera crew actually film all this as it was happening? They all said yes, It really did happen, you decide. Now is our Jesus Christ a Rebel Angel, the Messiah? will the Jewish people Now accept what I am saying as the Truth? was there any real Jewish people actually watching this as it happened? Be cool if a well-known

Jewish Rabbi actually was there watching all this, could there be? Could the Jewish People send a well-known Rabbi to listen to this lecture, to maybe standup at the right opportune time and tell this is all a Hoax? Can the film crew actually film some of the students wearing the black hat or maybe with the Jewish hair braids watching this all? It's kind of up to the Producer and Director of this film you are just reading the book. Could Luke actually write that He saw the Spirit of God go into Joseph and not the Virgin Mary? Someone did see this. Someone did see the Holy ghost go into the virgin Mary so is this Holy Ghost another male entity? What would we gain by saying the Spirit of God went into the virgin Mary AND the Holy Spirit went into the virgin Mary so are both Males? or maybe a God and a Goddess? Why would God pick Joseph again, knowing He was from the right bloodline of the Tribe of Judah with the right DNA to bring forth the Messiah then not use him, did an Angel actually tell Joseph to not lay with the virgin Mary? Is this what the Jewish people, in charge want you to read so they can prove this guy is not their Ha Mashiach? They had to kill Jesus to silence him they were willing to let a known Murderer go free so Jesus would be killed to silence him. To me it makes sense that God did choose Joseph, knowing He did have the right bloodline from the Lion of Judah and the Spirit of God did go into Joseph. The Holy Spirit or the Shekinah, wife of God went into the virgin Mary. Joseph was told to lay with his wife in the Physical sense and a baby was created. In the Spiritual sense, the God and Goddess did have sex also at the same time and this human flesh and blood mortal baby was created as the Son of a carpenter with the right bloodline from the lion of Judah, and the son of our God with the right bloodline to be the Ha Mashiach no laws of Deuteronomy 22 were broken yes a child was born in Bethlehem with the right blood line from the tribe of Judah and the tribe of Levi but the Jewish People had a good scam going and they had to silence this Rebel child and keep these 8 secrets hidden behind locked doors till the time was right. Is this the time? Is the world ready for the 8 secrets? The rest you know you decide." next scene. Next day, its early morning the old man gets a fresh cup of coffee sets down in his living room, Brigette and the camera crew set up, drink their coffee, everything is casual, kind of laid back, everyone is friendly, they have a Job to do, and the old man has a message to share with the world. now he talks: "You have hundreds and hundreds different Christian church's out there most are taught that now its ok to worship on Sunday the 1st day of the week. because Paul said it and you believe it show me anywhere in any holy bible were Jesus, while he was alive ever went to a church on Sunday, you can't, because Jesus was a good Jewish Hebrew who kept the ten commandments. Now there are some Christian church's that do keep the 7th day sabbath and some do keep the kosher food laws. they are realizing two of the secrets Jesus was sharing and that is good. What if I tell you that the Holy Bible teaching you that you are saved by Grace is wrong? What if I tell you this is just another ploy the Lucifer wanted to make you thank you are not accountable? If you are saved by Grace, then why is there a Judgement Day? When you die and your mortal, flesh and blood body does go back to a female and your Spirit does go before this Great white throne Judgement Day, yes, every knee shall bow, every tongue shall confess, you don't get to tell God that the Preacher told me I was saved by grace, It does not work that way. I will repeat this over and over because you need to understand this is one of the secret Teachings Jesus was trying to share with anyone willing to listen. Now people look at themselves backwards. They assume they are a mortal flesh and blood temporary human who happens to have somewhere Inside of them a Spirit/Soul. They were taught this way. What if all you know Is what you were taught? Your subconscious will only accept what you tell It to believe in. They can only teach you what they were taught, and their subconscious will only accept what they tell it to believe in. It's not your fault. Now you will get the opportunity to know the truth. Remember It took the Spirit world over 40 years to explain all this to me. It was hard for me to tell others I was a male Witch that sounded lame and Feminine to me so if I say I am a Warlock, not a male witch then that sounds tougher. Here I am trying to tell you 40 years of knowledge crammed in a short book, yes It will be overwhelming to some, others will accept and realize what all they were doing wrong. What works for one person may not work for another. Think about this, what If you are a doctor or Counselor, then you were trained in school to help others. Once you realize someone has a problem then with your training you would tell them what you would do, If you were them. the problem Is, you are not them. What works for you may not work for them, or another person. What works for one person may not work for another person. you see we all have a different fingerprint, with a different genetic makeup with a different DNA, etc. We think of Solomon in the Old Testament with hundreds of wives and concubines and as a male we think, well that is ok. Now if a female had hundreds of husbands and or consorts, we would think of her as a whore, a slut or a bitch, why? Its ok for a male to do this but not a female. So, when Father and Mother died and the world time changed from Bc to ad then we want to think that was all about Jesus the new male son of our God, but we do not mention the female in this creation process, again why? Our male ego, our male testosterone is telling us we are superior then a female. God did plant the seed but did a male God actually create anything? We want to think of Wicca as a pagan religion and burn these witches at a stake for thinking they had any Equality in this game we call life 101 For the last two thousand years our female, the Goddess and Daughters had to hide and became the Wicca Religion, but they did the same thing as the male Dominate religions did, there are no Equality. I went thru the 3 initiations of wicca, yes now you have a Dominant female Goddess as the creator. During the Spring she allows a Consort, a lover to come, plant his seed ,then grows and in the winter dies off and the next spring a new lover, a new consort arrives and plants his seed so the male species does not like it, but if a male species did this then it would b ok a male species is allowed to have many lovers then the Islam teach if you kill yourself and as many as you can them their God, Allah will give you 12 virgins, must be true, Allah says so. I apologize, again I am getting off track rambling on and on. Originally our God and Goddess told us there are certain foods we can eat and certain foods we should not eat, this is the Kosher food laws of Leviticus in the Old Testament. What if deep down we know that pork is a scavenger food and that to eat it you have to cook it at a certain temperature to kill these bacteria, does the dead bacteria just go away? No, it is still there, you are still eating it, hopefully it is all dead. I heard of Horror stories of people eating pork not cooked properly and the bacteria going into their blood stream and lodging in various parts of the body, Like the woman who had a brain tumor, she was getting dizzy spells so the doctors ran all kinds of tests on her and realized because she ate uncooked pork that bacteria grew in her brain the size of a golf ball giving her dizzy spells, They had to shave her beautiful hair and cut a hole in her brain to remove the Tumor and she had to go thru Chemo-therapy because of this which made her sick, all because of not obeying God's Laws of Kosher foods. I am temporary stuck in this mortal flesh and blood, human body so I can feed, eat, drink, experience the things I need to do during this lifetime, so you are what you eat, if you eat fat greasy foods, you become a fat greasy person, If you eat lean healthy foods then you become a lean healthy person, it's not rocket science its common sense. yes, I do have a immortal Spirit/Soul, yes I am what you would call a vampire. I do not drink blood, that is all Hollywood Movie hype to scare children and protect us from your stupidity. I absorb your power, your energy, some call us psychic vampyres, yes, I can touch you and absorb your energy like a vacuum. I can draw your energy, your power, just Like a prostitute will not only take your money from you, but they will also take your lifeforce, your orgasm and leave you drained, sometimes smiling and wanting to come back for more. Not everyone has an Immortal Spirit/ Soul. yes, some are just here just like animal, birds and fish, just here to live so many years, Experience what they need to experience then they die. You came from a female in this creation process and will someday return to a female. You call Her "Mother Earth". Next scene next act "Now it is time to tell a story. Elusive treasure or what if number one, Is the fact God does have a wife, you call Her the Holy Ghost, I Call Her the Shekinah, the Queen of Heaven, the Holy Ghost, the first-born daughter was Auriel, you call Her Mother Earth, She is the Comforter. You were taught as a Christian that there is a Male God, a new male son of God, Jesus Christ and a third male You call the Holy Spirit, so now who is this third male entity? The only Male who has that power is Lucifer, like it or not, yes, long before Jesus Christ was born and the New Testament was written, long before Moses was born and the Old Testament was written, long before Adam and Eve and this world was created. We know there was a Male God and a Female Goddess, they had many children, we know this because we call them Arch angels, now the real first born was Lucifer, the only person having the power to start a rebellion End of chapter 10

Vampyre

The sun doesn't bother me and neither does the cross,   for there is one God, Yahweh, who created me,   and we know He is the boss.   My spirit soul does live on forever,

thru each life it must end
I can remember and go in my past
or at times I just pretend,
I do sleep in a coffin, if the moon is right,
I can travel thru time, feelings of the sight.
I know there are other kindred spirits
that are out there just like me,
for the president of every company and
corporation are vam-powers for don't you see,
for they climbed that corporate ladder,
working and taking all the way to the top,
and no one knows where they are going,
and when and if they would ever stop.
for it is a hunger, that's in the blood,
the never-ending story, the denial if we could.
The sun it doesn't bother me
and neither does the cross,
for there is one God, Yahweh, who created me,
and we know He is the boss.   Copyright 2006
<u>www.poetry.com</u> by Melvin Abercrombie

act 11scene 11 episode 11

The old man is talking again   "we talked about this already but needs repeating again, what If you Imagine everyone in the world, millions. billions, trillions of people, all on this great big circular staircase, what if you all are Immortality, all immortal spirit souls? " I pause, take a drink of coffee then go on: "you look up and see a lot of people higher up then you, but now you understand, maybe they are older or know things you do not know, maybe you graduated from high school and maybe they have a college degree, maybe an Associate or Bachelor degree, maybe way up there they have the doctor's degree, You can look down and see there are people lower than you, Maybe they do not have their high school diploma or they are younger than you are. You do not know it but there are a lot of people on the same step you are on because you are, maybe in Texas, they may be In New York, California or Japan?" again, I pause take another drink of coffee then go on"

Now you can come back in five years and see
that some people are still on the same step. They
are not going up or down but happy were they are
at, Is this wrong? again I pause to show I am out
of coffee, so I get Up pour myself another cup,
set back down and continue:" So now you know
another story is the circular staircase, It's hard to
visualize millions of people all on a circular
staircase, but try to visualize me at the very top,
yes I was soaring with the eagles. I had
everything, the guy with the silver spoon or really
a gold spoon. then one night I was out where I
should not have been, yes, I was wild and crazy
drunk, I drove my custom van home. I had
money, I could call my limo driver to drive me
Home, it was three o'clock in the morning and my
stupid pride said You can do this. my ego when I
am drunk is a different person, I dozed off for only
a second, going 70 mph down the freeway I hit
the edge of a bridge and the van flipped over on
its side. Now you sober up real fast. You realize
there are no brakes and no steering You are
going down the road 70 mph and your van is
flipped over the gas tank is on your side and is
naturally pouring out and the van is on fire. you
try to open the passenger door to climb out and
you did not push It far enough, so the door comes
back and knocks you back into the van and the
fire. You realize then you are going to die they
say at the end, your whole life flashes before you,
yes, that is true. In my moment of despair, I cried
out, help me God, I do not want to die. a voice
told me to try again, this time i pushed the door
open and climbed out the same voice said run
and do not look back, I looked anyway to see my
custom van explode, the gas tank did that, fire
shot up 40 feet and knocked me down I rolled
over on fire and tried to put myself out. A truck
driver came and with his small fire extinguisher
he put my clothes out and took me to a hospital I
had to call my wife to come pick me up. I spent
the next three weeks in a VA hospital recovering
from all the burn, what is the secret about this?
What is the elusive treasure or secret here? I

was soaring with eagles, yes thru my pride, my ego, I was way up on top of the circular staircase. I lost everything for you see that was the straw that broke the camel's back, my wife left me, took our kids and went home to her family, I was stuck in a hospital for three weeks of agony and pain. but I feel I needed to experience these things, again I can write a book about all this, but I needed to experience these things firsthand." I pause for a moment get a fresh drink in hand and continue: " I like to tell motivational stories, some you have to figure out, could this be one of the secrets? You were told I may only reveal one secret a day but then on the other hand It's my life, who knows I may not be around for the next ten days, no one Is promised tomorrow" The camera goes to Rex who is setting next to Jasmine watching and protecting as Rex now speaks: "Long ago the old man had me install cameras in every room and record everything going on. that was His way of knowing what was going on in His house, every room, Butlers, maids all staff including my room and Jasmine's room. he also put me in charge of protecting Him so I have the same camera's in my room to monitor everything so yes I watched the bathroom scene of him flying around and I knew he was in no danger from any Physical being, He knows I am watching and all he has to say is Rex come here and I would be there in a Instance, the last 20 years I have been like a son to him and he is my father, we have no secrets, He knows about the Love I share with Jasmine, He thinks to himself, remembering as his hand shape-shifted in this demonic hand with long fingernails as he grabbed the edge of the bathroom sink, are the fingerprints left, his or some other demonic entity? I have been trained and watched enough movies and real life to understand that if this was a crime scene then they would dust for fingerprints and any found would be put in the data base, everyone knows this." He grabs his coffee cup and takes a drink, " People are unaware of the ghost camera, for you see no one can see the ghost camera, Is it a ghost? The presence running the lone camera feels to be another female, yes young you see a glimpse of her every once in a while". Rex continues:" Now he has the power He can now see her more clearly. the other film crew are unaware of the ghost camera filming all the behind-the-scenes activity. They set up In the living room He always wanted to get into the movie business and that was what these four young people chose. You have to start out doing minor task learning the ropes, same with any trade or business. you cannot just go up there and tell them you want your high school diploma or bachelor's degree you have to take the time and earn it. Just like in the Army you can't just go up there and say you want to be a General, again you have to earn it. So now the old man wonders about this new power he has, Will this demon appear again? Will his hands or other parts of his body shape shift into this demonic creature? What about the raven wings one was broken, yes, he felt the pain coursing thru his body as if you broke a leg, the excruciating pain he did feel, was it his Imagination? He felt the blood pouring down his back as he curled up on the floor, was all this his imagination? Yes, the pride, the vanity, the arrogance He felt the power as the wings did lift him off the floor. He felt alive and younger, much stronger but only for a moment. He now understood the power of the angels and demons if only for a moment He still tasted the power and felt it go thru out all of His body He was alive only for a moment and now all He has is the memory" but how did you turn off the bathroom light by just waving your hand? he will practice after everyone leaves and see if he still has this power, time will Tell, What will he do with this gift? Is it a gift from God or the Goddess, Lucifer or some Demonic force? If he can shapeshift into this demonic entity, can he shape-shift into something else? So far only his hands seem to change will other parts of his body change also? he felt this power surge thru him sort of like when the Wings grew on his Back he felt the power, he could actually fly, if only for a moment, he obviously felt what the angels and demons must have felt. yes, the power was sensational, the energy was great, He felt the power, if only for a moment and he will have that to remind him at what cost? He will not forget the other power, when lightning broke His wing off, everyone heard it snap and He felt the pain. He said: "I do not want to go thru that again, never again". Now that I told you a story You have to ask yourself did this really happen right before we got here. Or could this have happened a long time ago and the old man is playing with our Imagination? Does the old man have a lot of tattoos? Or is this just another wild dream?" The two camera Crew and Brigette looked at each other to see what each one thought about it. Smiling the old man said, "ok I will take off my shirt, you will see me running around In my bathing suit sooner or later so we need to get this over now". The camera crew filmed the old man taking off His shirt and revealing his many tattoos all over His chest and upper arms. no one in public has ever seen Him without a shirt, yes, he was the multi-billionaire who was a motivational speaker, people paid thousands of dollars to hear one of his seminars. He was always so professional three-piece suit and tie and He had nice gray hair, so they were surprised to see a shaven bald headed younger version of all the pictures of him they have seen. Next act next scene   she clips a microphone to my shirt, and they say, "anytime you are ready", the film starts up as he sets on the couch. "We already talked about some of my elusive treasures like Merlyne and my Immortality and our Goddess, the hidden Queen and me going thru some trials and tribulations as teaching me. You can write a book about these things but sometimes we have to go thru these things to experience them and teach us some ways toward Enlightenment.so our circular staircase and maybe the story of me sprouting demonic wings and shape shifting can be treasure number two and some people may see thirteen or fourteen treasure's out of the book or movie, Some of my secrets you may already have heard but I am telling you again so I will add a few extra ok?" I paused took a drink then went on " I want to share a little more info as it comes to me, I hope you realize I am only saying all the what ifs that pops up in my mind or What I feel It tells me to, so one moment I will talk about one thing then all of a sudden out of the blue, talk about something else, remember this. I realize getting a lot of different people to come together under one Church or Religion is farfetched. What if we could get a million people to at least read this book, would the world be a better place? What if a million people now understand what this is all about. I do believe there are a lot of people out there who for various reasons are not happy with the Religion and Church they were taught. All you know is what you were taught I said it before and I will keep on saying it, If you are not happy with the Church or Religion you were Taught then you do have the right to go looking for another. I looked for over twenty years, trying to find God, Then I realized there has to be a female Creator in this process. As a Male Species I can see why a lot of males do not want woman to have equal rights, they want to run things. If the average person would be happy as equal, then we would not have a problem but give some woman power and It goes to their head. I see some woman when you give them a badge, a gun and police authority it goes to their head and they are very mean, yes, they are dealing with Inmates, bad boys and bad girls, yes, they broke the law but they are still human beings with feelings and emotions, On the other hand, I seen some woman glad to have the power and treat all as equal. Again, all you know is what you were taught, maybe a man at one time did abuse you and I understand that, sometimes we need to learn the hard way and it's the learning process we all are constantly going thru Its the same with some men, give them a badge and gun and it will

go to their heads also. it works both ways. That is
another reason I believe Immortality Cowboy
Church Is a good thing, It gives a lot of different
people from all walks of life the opportunity to join
together under one roof to meet and talk about
our culture differences. I also believe in the
kosher food laws, The Jewish, Islam and some
Christians do not eat pork, catfish, lobster or
shrimp, these are still called "Scavenger foods" I
will try to teach people the importance of this,
some will still want to eat whatever they want to,
yes, they are Rebels too, but most once they
realize the bacteria and germs then hopefully
refrain from eating unclean scavenger foods. I
grew up as a Baptist. My grandpa raised pigs, so
I grew up eating pork. Some of my families are
still stubborn Baptist and still eat pork. I found out
there is turkey bacon, turkey ham and turkey
sausage so it's better for me. I still sometime eat
good ole pork bacon or a pork chop, is God going
to put me in a burning hell forever and ever? Do I
take the risk of this germs spreading thru out my
body and become a tumor or a cancer? you
decide you now know what is good for you and
what is not. I am still waiting on turkey pork chop,
but until then I will eat lamb chops which are very
good." the sexy voice says:" New clothes, new
scene new part of the series we are now in the
largest church in Texas, thousands of people
here to listen to the old man speak about this
Holy Grail and Immortality cowboy Church
Ministry the one church that the Rebel Jesus
would actually go to. The audience settles down
as the camera scans over the area and the old
man speaks: " We know in the beginning our God
and our Goddess did create Adam and Eve and
this World in six days and we know then God
rested on the 7th day. This is Friday night and all-
day Saturday You can look at any dictionary at
the word Saturday and the definition will say it's
the 7th day of the week, look at any calendar to
verify this, also now look up the word Sunday in a
dictionary and again you will see that Sunday is
the first day of the week, Monday is the second

day of the week and Tuesday is the third day of the week, etc. Some religions do keep this 7th day of the week as the sabbath, there are many Christian groups that do still keep the Kosher food laws and the 7th day Saturday sabbath, Most Christians, however feel like they are no longer under the law and worship Jesus Christ on Sunday because He arose from the grave on Sunday, the 1st day of the week, what if they are wrong? Even in His death He could not break the Law and He waited till the 7th day Saturday sabbath was over to arise from the grave. During the 33 years that Jesus Christ was a live He never worshipped on Sunday the 1st day of the week, He always kept the 7th day Saturday sabbath and he told us in 1john If you love me then keep my Commandments, so this is commandment number four. But Paul says now we are no longer under the Law, Is Paul a Rebel? He is telling you we are no longer under the law so that sounds like a Rebellion to me? so are you a follower of Paul or Jesus? What about the commandment "thou shall not kill, or thou shall not steal are we under these Commandments? Yes, you say so now do we get to pick which commandment we want to be under and which one we do not have to obey, sounds like another form of rebellion to me." He stops talking as the noise is heard, Then the back door opens as the most beautiful woman starts walking down the Aisle, she turns and waves her hands as again all the doors locked. Different people see her as what they love in a woman, to some she is blonde hair, tall with blue eyes, to others she is a fiery red head with emerald, green eyes, what is she to you? She sprouts beautiful angel wings and flies around the church as the audience is amazed at all her beauty, yes this is Auriel, first born daughter of our God and Goddess, you call Her Mother Earth or Mother Nature, sister of Lucifer or now who calls himself Georgio. She flies up to the stage as i hand her the microphone, shaking and trembling I fall on my knees again knowing her power. Talking in the microphone she says

"Ok settle down I am Auriel, first born daughter of
our Father God and Mother Goddess, you have
called me Mother Earth or Mother Nature, yes
that is true. my brother Lucifer, who now likes to
call himself Georgio, the Rebel Angel you have
already met and I too have stood back and
watched you pathetic humans make a mockery
out of our Religions, Finally we allowed this man"
stopping she puts her hand out to pull me back
up then smiling she says" Melvin Abercrombie
who in a past life was called Merlyne and now
you know him as a male Witch or a Warlock, who
is also teaching you about the Psychic Vampyres
or the real Vampires to write the books that will
teach you the path to Avalon Fishermen church
ministry, the one true church That I approve of.
We need Rebel Angels to show this pathetic
world the truth about religions. We need people to
stand up and admit they are a Warlock or a
Vampyre, come out of the closet, it's not just
about the gays and lesbians. You have the right
to search your religion, you have the right to ask
questions and demand answers, so yes listen to
this man, read his books tell others who he is, for
He has my blessings too. so Yes i approve of
these and the eight teachings of bringing back
our Mother, Re-incarnation, the kosher food laws,
The 7th day Saturday sabbath and you are not
saved by grace, Jesus is your Jewish Messiah,
Jesus did not die for your sins and now creating a
Immortality Cowboy Church were even my
brother Lucifer accepts as the true church are
correct, so now you will have my blessings also"
She puts her arm around me, I am shaking, with
tear filled eyes, trying to smile, she walks away,
and the doors all unlock and now she is gone. I
grab the microphone and say "Wow, I do not
know what to do think about that for now, End of
Chapter 11

Disagreement again

.   "The scent of a Woman", driving me wild,
sometimes I am an adult, sometimes I am a child.
The smell of earth beneath my feet,

my head on her bosom, the feel of her heartbeat.
the wind in my hair, the smell of burnt wood,
tells me a campfire is going, if only I could,
find her for now it is starting to rain,
the thunder, lightning, only adds to the pain
of memories of yesterday, words that were said,
cuts like a knife, thru living and dead.
We sometimes speak and say without thinking,
cruel, mean words, then without blinking,
we add fuel to the fire by saying more,
until one or the other runs out the door.
Then alone, with time contemplating the words,
then realizing how stupid and so absurd,
you run after, willing to apologize, but then
she is not there, gone like the wind.
You run, look, cry out her name,
as tears start to fall, to cover the shame,
"The scent of a Woman" driving me wild,
sometimes I am a adult, sometimes I am a child.
Copyright 2006 www.poetry.com by Melvin
Abercrombie

act 12 scene12 episode 12   The old man is

speaking, so now do you remember your first
love?" He Looks around at everyone shaking their
heads In agreement" How about your first kiss?"
again they all nod their head" for me It was a long
time ago yes I was going thru my puberty a time
when little boy's wake up with a hard on and go to
bed with a hard on" They all laugh and smiling
they nod their heads smiling back I continue " I
was twelve and in the sixth grade back then I had
a lot of thick red hair and freckles" Smiling he
rubbed his bald head everyone laugh's as he
continued " Hardly any girl ever noticed me yes
my family were rich but they wanted me to go to a
public school and they hid this from them, they
thought the butler who picked me up In the old
station wagon was my dad, It was my secret, dad
was off In Europe somewhere making big million
dollar deals .then one day out of the blue the
prettiest girl in school, Peggy sue walked over to

me, beautiful blonde hair and big blue eyes. She looked at me and said do you want to be my friend? My heart was pounding ninety miles an hour and I got this tremendous erection" Everyone is laughing, as I hold my hand up, smiling trying to continue "Yes, I was embarrassed hoping she would not look down and notice and take off running, she didn't, and I was relieved. She held my hand and said you will be my knight in shining armor to protect me from evil fire breathing dragons. Yes, I was willing to be any one she wanted me to be. Now I know what your first love is all about, my heart was beating so fast, the excitement, The goose bumps from her holding my hand then she looks around to see If anyone was watching, she let go of my hand then with both of her hands she touched my face, then kissed me. I guess she saw her daddy kiss her mom that way It was over in a moment, but I can still taste that sweet ness of that first kiss." I stopped for a moment to take a drink then went on " She said' do you want to get on the seesaw?" "Yes" I replied willing to go anywhere or do anything she wanted to I weighed more than she did so I could Tell I had to take it easy as I went down I would stretch out my feet to slow down the bend and push back up ever so gently She was smiling yes she was happy. I guess every school has their bully and this elementary school was no exception he failed school twice, so he was much older and fatter. no one Liked him because If he seen you bringing your lunch he would grab it, eat all your cupcakes or desert and push you around. He came over to my side of the seesaw and said for me to get off. He put his foot to keep the seesaw from moving i looked over at her she was way up in the air, and she was shaking her head no, she did not want to play with him. I told him "No, go away" with his left hand he grabbed a head full of my red hair, yes It hurt. He had rotten teeth and bad breath as he showed me his right hand, then got into my face and said "Ok punk, do you want a black eye? A broke nose? or a busted lip?" Trembling

not knowing what to do, I panicked I got up and
he sat down peggy started screaming he said "Its
ok I am not going to hurt you, he pushed up real
fast then as he came down, he moved his legs,
so he hit with a thud. I thought she was going to
fly thru the air. She kept on screaming as they
went up and down. I stood back in horror. I was
supposed to be her Knight in shining armor and
slay the mean evil fire breathing dragon. She was
Guinevere the damsel in distress I was helpless.
Our small English teacher came out telling the big
bully to stop. he took one look at her small body
and laughing kept on. As he came down with a
thud, she stepped on the seesaw holding it down
with her foot. with her left hand she grabbed his
right ear and twisted it as hard as she could, in
pain he lashed out with his right hand and she
grabbed it and twisted It around he started
standing and I ran over to grab the seesaw as he
got off and started fighting her I let the seesaw
down easy so peggy could get off. she hung on to
his ear with one hand and twisted his right arm
around his back as he turned around, she kicked
him as hard as she could right behind his knee,
and he went down. another male teacher who
saw It all from a distance came running over, took
the bully into the principal office and he got a
good spanking. back then If you misbehaved then
you did get a good spanking. I ran over to Peggy
Sue who was crying, thru her tears she said " I
thought you were my knight In shining armor?
You were supposed to rescue me from all the fire
breathing dragons, but you did not. You are not
my friend no more. I do not like, you go away" I
was devastated. You are only a kid, no one tells
you what to do. knowing now I should have taken
some martial art classes, which I did later on.
maybe I could have done something different
everyone knows woulda shoulda coulda, now I
play this scenario back in my mind, when he
grabbed my hair with his left hand that left his left
side vulnerable. If you raise your left arm up then
feel the tender spot under your arm" I paused
took a drink and could see everyone raising their

left arm to see what I was talking about and they shaking their heads in agreement now understanding that is a vulnerable spot I continue." With my left elbow I could hit him as hard as i could like this" showing everyone a basic karate blow using my left elbow hitting his imaginary chest." now he would definitely let go of my hair. In pain his right hand would still aim for my face. So, remember the movie Karate Kid" I pause look at everyone they shake their Head I take another drink then go on "wax on wax off" what if I sway my right arm up to block his on-coming blow. Now I grab His right arm with both of my hands and do the same thing the small teacher did. Yes, she was small, but She did take some self-defense classes and It paid off when the big fire breathing dragon tried to fight her. Of course, I was humiliated and embarrassed, A small woman fought this mean bully and made a fool out of me. It was not her fault. I am glad she came along I needed to learn a lesson. My first Love, my first kiss was over, Peggy Sue found another boyfriend. I often thought about If I did take some self-defense classes yes, my dad asked me was I ready for that and I told Him no What would it be like if I did take the Karate Classes and beat up the bully? I could have eventually married Peggy Sue and our children would be different, yes different names, different fingerprints, different facial qualities. I love my children and grandchildren These things happen for a reason. I needed to fall in love, have my heart broken 30 minutes later and now get to experience these things" I pause for a moment showing my coffee cup is empty, the Maids brought in some donuts, so we take a short break, their camera is off, but the lone camera Is still rolling showing all the behind-the-scenes activity. The camera goes to the boxing arena again showing the same beautiful girl in the bikini and showing the same big sign saying ten minutes later This time. everyone is amused. back to work, he sets down in his recliner The girls are ready they motion him to start whenever you are ready, he takes a drink of coffee and sets it on the coffee table then begins again " say for example you have two people in the army both are wearing the same green uniform, one is a Private and the other is a General , How do you tell the difference between the two? They are both wearing the same shirt, same Pants, Same boots and same Hats? One is a Private and the other is a General how do you tell the difference? We all Know they have these little medals on the Private has a one bar chevron and the General has a chrome star, this is how you know which person to salute and show respect to." We stop and take another break this time for lunch their camera stops but the lone camera keeps going she does not need to take a break; she does not eat or drink or go to the bathroom like we do. She is a Spirit/Soul that thrives off of energy. Just like a vampire drinks blood to survive She is one of the original VamPowers who thrive off your power or energy, yes, she can go into human form into another physical mortal flesh and blood human to temporary experience, feed, drink, and absorb your energy, sometimes thru the sexual act during intercourse draining the orgasm from Her victims, the lifeline of all creation. they lay their smiling, drained and all energy gone not realizing were all the Energy went to. They have to go to sleep to re-charge themselves then go thru the process over and over not knowing what is going on. The blind sheep, who is the predator?" next act next scene To Keep this from being a boring movie or a boring book you can Imagine as the old man Is talking maybe he is wearing different costumes, remember He is very rich and crazy, so he likes to dress up or down according to his latest feelings and emotions. maybe disguised as someone or something different to keep the excitement going, the old man talks: " You have a right to ask what if questions and demand what if answers, you have a right to form your own immortality church Ministry and have other speakers teach you what you want to learn. Would the world be a better place if your typical

Christian actually learned about Buddha, Hindu, Islam and Jewish teachings? You have this illusion you only get one chance at this game called life and you get to go to a heaven or a hell forever and ever, Will there be Islam there? What about Buddha? Hindu? or other denominations, again all you know is what you were taught, who gets to say your religion is right and all the other religion is wrong? Would the world be a better place if we all would learn a little about other religions, then decide what is right for us.? What may be right for you, may not be right for me, my favorite color is red, so everyone who likes red can join my church, your favorite color maybe blue, sorry you are not invited, you have to go down the street and start your own blue church, some of the doctrines are that simple. then you have a hundred shades of red, so now you have more Rebel denominations and more "versions" of the Holy Bible and more different Rebel Church's on each corner, ok so now let's tell another story, a long time ago there was a tribe of people, there was no such thing as money they Had animals and other things as value to trade so when the Chief decided his son was ready to become a man and get married he thought he was old enough and was taught well to handle his own life so he gave him ten cows out of his herd. Now the value is, it starts with the lowest which is chickens, then pigs, sheep and cows as the highest so you figure so many chickens will buy a pig and so many sheep would be equal to a cow, so they traded to survive. One of the cows was actually a male bull who has the power to get all the cows pregnant at different times to have baby calves and let the flock grow. Now when a woman reaches the age to be married, she is put Inside a circle so all the eligible man can see her as she turns each man has the power to bid on her and the highest price is the winner, she does have the option of looking at the highest bidder and turn away If she so chooses and the next bidder gets the chance. Only when she reaches out to him and accepts the bid then they both become married, kind of like a dowry. The son of the chief was in love with this young woman and they both knew a day would come when she would have to be bid upon. When the woman went down to the river to wash their clothes, they would brag about what their husbands gave for them, one would say my husband gave two pigs and three chickens for me, another one laughing would say that is nothing my husband gave two cows and one sheep for me, the stories went on and On. When her day came only the eligible man formed the circle and the chief said ok, we will start the bidding. before anyone else had the chance to stand up the son of the chief stood up and said, "I will give All ten of my cows for her". The chief was surprised and so was everyone else no one has ever given that many cows for one woman It was unheard of. Even the woman blushed and looked at him smiling she put out her hands to accept and everyone cheered. Yes, they were married all the other man said we all knew she was for you, and you could have gotten her for a lot less. No one else would bid against you. He turned and looked at his future wife and spoke. I know I just wanted her and every-one else to know that I love her so much I was willing to give everything for her. The story of the ten-cow woman spread for thousands of years yes, he slowly built up his worth again and people still talk about how love can solve all problems. Sometimes you must be willing to give everything for what you want and let the world know that some people learn this secret or is it an elusive treasure? and apply it to their own lives It's up to you" That's It for the day, may-be tomorrow another secret now relax jump in the pool or ocean eat and go over the film footage. Next act next scene " another story i call the winning Edge is not just about sports or who get the trophy or blue ribbon. the Winning Edge is an attitude, once you realize most of us were taught it does not matter who wins or loses it's how you play the game. This is the game we call life, yes you are in it and will be from the day you were born until the day you die. you realize there are two kinds of people rich and poor, the predators and the victims so who are you? The 1% controlling the 99% the difference between a rich person and a poor person is the rich person has the winning edge attitude and will never ever give up, they may lose everything but go back knowing they will achieve and win in the end I talked about the different parts of the body wanting to be the boss. the brain said I should be the boss because I have the brain, the heart said I should be the boss because I have a good heart, the eyes said, well I see, the ears said, well, I can hear, the arms legs and lungs all argue about they should be the boss, finally the ass hole said I should be the boss, so they all started laughing and the ass hole shut up. Finally, the brain started getting dizzy the heart and lungs felt the pressure the eyes and ears did too, and the arms lungs and legs could hardly move finally they all gave in and made the asshole the boss. The moral of the story is a boss can have a good brain, heart, eyes, ears lungs, arms and legs but sometimes the boss has to be an asshole. When i was a electrician they made me the foreman, I had twenty people working under me and I had to hire and fire people so at times I was called an ass-hole but the bottom line the company depended on me to get the job done. the worse part was when the owner came out and said we have no more work and will have to let ten of your guys go its lay off time, so I had to lay off ten good men who had wife and children and depended on them so yes, I was a asshole that day. Another story I remember seeing these statues and paintings of a baby Angel many, many baby angels or cherubs so I wondered if a baby angel ever grew up to be a teenage angel? will they grow up to be an adult Angel? will they ever get married and create more baby angels the way we do? We think of our God as an old gray-haired man, with a long gray beard, so is God old? Does God ever die like we do? Can God live the 2 thousand years which is the zodiac sign of

change? We know while Jesus was alive, we were in the zodiac sign of Pisces the fish. Now we are in the age of Aquarius the water bearer so when time changed from B.C. to A. D. Did God and Goddess die, and a new cycle, rebirth and circle was created? We know Lucifer, the first born is ruling now and that is why we are divided, we are very scattered and confused we went from 7 Gods to a 6 Gods then 5 Gods and the Christians say only 3 Gods that are all male. Immortality Cowboy church, worships only one God, Yahweh and one Goddess Shekinah as equal. Yes we accept the teachings of the Rebel Angel, Lucifer and the 4 guardians and Jesus Christ, you have this illusion when you die and get to go to heaven forever and ever you will see that one religion one church so you can wait till you die and find out the truth or wake up and realize the equality now." next act next scene
The old man is talking: "the next elusive treasure is, You are not saved by grace, Some church's teach you, You can do whatever you want to, Go out and kill twenty or a hundred people, steal or break all the laws and right before you die all you have to do is say the three magic words and you get to go to heaven forever and ever, So now you are asking what are the three magic words right? " I pause, look around then continue "the three magic words are "God Forgive Me" They teach you that you are saved by grace, but God teaches that "Every Knee Shall Bow and Every Tongue Shall Confess" Yes there is a Judgement Day. You came from   a Female, when you were born and when you die you will go back to a female, We call her Mother Earth, If our forefathers want to call her Persephone the Goddess of the underworld and put a statue of Her on top of our white house capitol building for all the world to see, then who are we to argue with that? Yes, She Is Auriel, guardian of the north your true circle will open in the North, your mortal, flesh and blood human body Will die, You can pay the funeral home a lot of money for a fancy casket, embalming fluid and a concrete

vault, you are only making them rich and prolonging the Inevitable They are laughing at you all the way to the bank, your Spirit/Soul left your body and is judged are you going to tell God and the Goddess that you were saved by Grace? It does not work that way. I do believe that Jesus Christ Is on the right-hand side of God and will speak on your behalf, yes, I was born a Christian I was saved and baptized and believe Jesus Christ is the son of God, but so Is the rebel Angel Satan or Lucifer. I still accept the teachings of Jesus Christ and want to learn the teachings of Buddha and the Hindu teachings Is that so bad? What is the difference between a rich person and a poor person? The rich person never gives up, He keeps on trying over and over, Even If he loses everything, they have the knowledge that sooner or later they will finally achieve what they want. Which one are you? this time we are outside. We have a swimming pool with a manmade waterfall pumping water out of the pool and circulating back in and adding the chlorine as needed. This is our little picture of the garden of Eden, it's a nice day so we decided to film outside. Everything is set up Brigette places the microphone on his shirt collar trying again to get him to look at her hard nipples but he is faithful to his wife so ready to go: " I always ask a lot of questions That is how you find out the answer even when I was a kid I always wanted to know things, dad bought me the latest encyclopedia and computers and private tutors to teach me all the things a rich child should know. One of the big questions we already asked was does God have a Fingerprint? We were created in the Image of a God so it would make sense that if He wanted to identify us by giving us a unique different Fingerprint then He would have one also. Does the Goddess, or the Female side of a God does She have a fingerprint? Does the sons and daughters, we call angels and demons have a fingerprint? so now If, when we die from our mortal, flesh and blood human body and we are Judged, do we carry this same fingerprint with us from one Re-incarnation to another? We know we have lived many past lives; I have gone into self-hypnosis and recall some of my previous lives. I was never a King or President or If I was, I do not remember, one past life I have had several dreams about, so they felt real did I leave my fingerprint in my dream? We know back in the time the black plague was going on and a lot of good people did die, all my family, my wife and children all did die from the black plague, why was I spared? I believed I was spared because during that time I studied the magical arts some were good magic and others were what was called dark magic I was a real Vampire which means I did not drink blood but absorb the energy the Power from my victims, you would now call us physic vampires ,for you see a real vampire never drinks blood, He or She is not afraid of the cross or the sun that is all Superstition to fool the common people. We can touch you and pull your energy from you. We can use our 5 senses and merely look at you and my eyes will touch you and I can draw your power from you. If I hear your voice say even on a telephone all the way across to Europe i can touch you thru my hearing. After all my family died from the black plague, I found solace in the bottle of rum to satisfy the demons inside of me only to wake up the next day, hungry and wanting to feed from a new victim and back to the bottle of rum to quiet the demons if only for a while. The people who ran the ships were having a hard time getting sailors to run their ships and the pirate trade were no different, one night a stranger bought me several rounds of rum and as I passed out, they Loaded me on their ship, the next morning I woke with a hangover far away from land. I had a choice, jump overboard and feed the sharks or work the boat. Not much of a choice but I wanted to live. They got into a fight with another ship and a man come running at me with a sword, I had to defend myself or die, I killed him, stole what he had on him including his nice sword and tossed his body over board to the sharks he would have done the

same for me, killing got easier, at the time I knew
killing was wrong I grew up as a Christian back
then and I knew sooner or later I will have to
make my peace with my God.. The ship
eventually was hit, and we all started sinking,
every man for himself the captain and a few of his
right-hand man grabbed the only few lifeboats i
found a door that was tore off because of the
cannon explosion and grabbed it hoping it would
float, it did. I fell asleep on the board and woke up
the next morning to a bright sunny day, no one in
sight, if anyone did survive, they were long gone.
I drifted for three days and three nights, delirious,
laughing that I am surrounded by all this food,
and I am starving, surrounded by all this water
and I was dying of thirst. I tried drinking the salt
water, it only made me sick, finally out of
desperation I called on this God and Goddess to
forgive me. I know I had no right to ask, but I
accepted my fate and too weak to stay on I rolled
off the board. A beautiful naked blonde woman
with blue eyes swam up behind me and rescued
me, even in my weakness I was aroused, she
was beautiful, I felt this must be heaven, I did not
deserve this, but I am not complaining, finally my
feet touched sandy bottom and I walked a shore I
turned to get the woman who helped me, she
waved and swam off, she was a mermaid, half
woman, half fish. I will never forget the dreams
over and over. It seemed so real. I made a vow to
change my ways and I became a preacher, trying
to teach others the amazing power of our creator
God and Goddess. Another past life I was an
outlaw, I was a very bad person who killed and
stole from people, this was during the 1800's. I
fell in Love with this beautiful red head, who
happened to be married to the town sheriff. One
night in a drunken brawl he shot me in the back,
to coward to face me, as I laid dying, she came
up to me and whispered in my ear that she was
pregnant with my child. My last words were to tell
him It is his so he will not hurt you. I made my
peace with my God, and I was judged, I was born
Inside the womb of the red head I was in love

with, yes now I became her red headed daughter, and she knew who I was in a previous life. I spent my whole life taking care of the woman who in one life was my lover and another life was my mother, stranger things have happened, I guess. The Sheriff was shot a short time later by another drunk who out drew him. Wait you ask what is the secret here? Just another story or what? Some may see another secret maybe they too have had past life regression there has to be something to this Re-incarnation. It makes sense. could the secret be if you are going into a self-hypnosis mode and telling your mind to go back in time to maybe a past life or maybe you are having a recurring dream you need the key to open this door maybe some other people can help you. Most Christian Churches were taught you have a male God, a new male son of God and another male entity, no one knows as the male Holy Spirit and that is your Trinity, It takes three of something to make a Trinity, right? Once again I ask the question if we go to Genesis chapter 6 then it says "the sons of God looked down and saw the daughters of men are fair and they took them wives and there were Giants in the land" so is this were the giants came from? maybe like Hercules and Atlas, half God and half mortal? we all know the story of David and Goliath so now, if God went directly into the virgin Mary then why was Jesus not a Giant? The Jewish wanted their Messiah to be a Giant, a man who could lead them into a powerful nation, Have you ever wondered why the Roman Empire who used a eagle as their symbol and they failed, then the Italians came to America and helped create the greatest nation using the same Eagle as their symbol and making sure the Capitol in Washington, where the President and all of congress work and put a female Goddess statue on top, could that be originally their Goddess Juno? Did God break his own laws of Deuteronomy22? It clearly says that God commanded these laws and if a woman was already promised to another man and someone had sex with her then that person would be stoned to death, if that woman did not cry out then she too would be stoned to death. it is obvious God chose Joseph to be her husband and God knew that Joseph was from the right bloodline of Judah, the Lion of Judah that would bring in this new Messiah under Gods own laws is he responsible? Should the virgin Mary be stoned also? What do you call a child born out of wedlock? That is what other religions think of our Christ, what else can they think all they know is what they were taught, Is Luke right? Or Is Luke only writing down what people tell him their "Version" of what they think actually did happen? Stop right now and read that. Now the truth, what really did happen Luke's version was written around 50ad almost twenty years after Christ was killed a lot of time has elapsed and the stories handed down. What if the Spirit of God actually did go into Joseph? Knowing he had the right bloodline from the Tribe of Judah and the right DNA to bring forth the true Messiah (Ha Mashiach) and the Holy Ghost, the Goddess, the wife of God did go into the Virgin Mary. God had sex with his wife in the spiritual world, Joseph had sex with his wife in the physical world There was no laws broken The marriage was legal, The child born was the son of a carpenter, a normal child, no giant, with the rightbBloodline from the Tribe of Judah, the lion of Judah, to bring forth the true Messiah(Ha Mashiach) and also more important the Son of God you have a choice accept Luke's version and believe that our Jesus cannot be the Messiah according to his "version" are accept maybe all Luke knows Is what he was taught also remember who would benefit by this? The same angel that told Eve it was ok to eat the forbidden apple, This Is his world like it or not, He is the ruler, you have a choice. The old man speaks again: " I have said a lot of things in this book over and over again, again why? so you the reader will remember only thru repetition will we remember things. We now realize that some believe the only reason God allowed Jesus to die was to get rid of the animal sacrificial law. Did the animal sacrificial law really go away because of Jesus' death? No, remember the Jewish people did not have a welfare system like we do today. there were no free food stamps, no free section 8 housing, so to help the needy, the sick, handicap and diseased people the church had to get money somehow, so the animal sacrificial law was one way, you commit a sin you feel guilty so you go to the church give a animal or money and the church says they will pray for you. the catholic learned this real fast and said just give me ten percent of your money and I will put in a good word for you and now say the 3 magic words God Forgive me and you get to go to heaven forever and ever. You do not give us ten percent then you will burn in a hell forever and ever and for two thousand years churches have made a lot of money off of stupid, gullible people. Was this a part of the Olde World Order? Did God, The Father look down and see people breaking his Laws and being told by the Rabbi's to go out and find an Innocent animal. a calf, a sheep or other animal, bring it to the Rabbi and they will pray over it and your sins will be atoned? Kind of like the catholic church, so now we know where the Catholic Church got that idea. Judas Iscariot knew that Yeshua was the Messiah, the Ha Mashiach and He knew his Jesus had the power to call a legion of angels down to save him at the last minute, you want to think of Judas as a betrayer of the Christ. Judas Loved the Messiah and was tired of running and decided to show the world the power Jesus did have. Judas did not betray Jesus. Judas turned him in, to show who he really was, the son of God, who had the power of getting a legion of Angels to come down and rescue him at the last minute, but Judas did not know that God, the father allowed his son to die to do away with the animal sacrificial Law. why should an Innocent animal die for something you done? What did the animal do wrong? Then the Jewish people changed from an animal to just money for your sins, thanks to lucifer. When

Judas saw his messiah die, then he had no choice but throw the thirty pieces of silver down and hang himself. If he would have waited, he would have seen the Messiah, come back alive, now with a short haircut and clean shaven so the people would not recognize him and walking along the road, to get out of that town and those people, then Thomas questioning him saying, I say the Christ being stabbed in the side, you look different, if you are the Christ, show me the wound, so Jesus did show him and now he is called doubting Thomas to this day. Jesus, his wife, Mary Magdalene and their children, two boys Jesus Jr and Jessie and she was pregnant with Sarah, Joseph, Mary the Virgin Mother of Jesus and all his brothers and sisters had to flee the area. Where did they go? Did Jesus just go up to a heaven forever and ever or did Jesus and their family go to different countries? We want to believe the Da Vinci code that the Bloodline of Jesus is still alive today. We want to believe, Jesus was married, had children and the bloodline is still going on, what about Jesus himself, did he just disappear in a heaven forever? Could Jesus go to the orient and influence the Buddha? could Jesus go to the middle east and influence the Islam and Hindu? we know the Mary Magdalene did go to Europe, France, England and other countries that have created a Mary Magdalene church but where is the Joseph church or the Virgin Mary Church? Is the catholic the only one? does any of their bloodline count as part of the Messiah? What about His other brothers and sisters do they count at all? We know Joseph, the carpenter, father to Jesus and the Virgin Mary did have many other children. We also know that Joseph, the carpenter was older and married before, so he had sons and daughters from a previous marriage, so these are only stepsons and stepdaughters of Jesus, not the same bloodline, where in the Da Vinci Code is the mother of Jesus, the Virgin Mary mentioned?? We are slowly evolving from a hundred different Christian denominations to just that one church, that one religion that Adam and eve actually went to. We can now call it a New World Order or go back two thousand years and go back to the Olde World order it is going to happen, evolution is happening, and the decline of Christianity and all the other so-called religions are happening. we have different race of people now freely inter breeding and we are not able to categorize humans the way we used to because now they are half white and half black or whatever. The gays and Lesbians have a free rein to do what-ever they what to and sexual behavior is in a worldwide crisis. Rome was not built over night and was not destroyed overnight, and it's the same with Christianity, Islam, Jewish, Buddha or whatever Religion you had in the past, its evolution like it or not call it a New World Order or go back to a Olde World Order whatever name you want to call it, does not matter. History does prove itself over and over again. We have a few people in charge, who want to control the majority. This has always been the case and always will as long as there are Demons and Angels among us controlling us. We can argue about this new world Order and see all the good parts of it and we can see all the bad parts of it, eventually we will wake up and realize we need to go back to the Olde World Order and see what the real Adam and eve actually did believe. This is the 7th teaching of the Yeshua Christus, but we want modern religion, we want to think no matter what I do I get to go to Valhalla forever and ever, or all we have to say is the 3 magic words "God Forgive me" and get to go to a Heaven forever and ever sorry It does not work that way. That is one of the reasons of the decline of Christianity is the illusions they cram down your throat. Think about this. Now another story, a guy said he could walk a tight rope blindfolded across Niagara Falls pushing a wheel barrel. Of course, this feat has never been done so no one believed him, His preacher told him it was very dangerous, and he would be killed, He looked the preacher in the eye and said you told me If I believed in the power of a mustard seed I could move a mountain, Well I do not want to move a mountain I believe I can do this. I want you to be there yes pray for me and be there on the other side when I get across, the preacher agreed. The man pushed the wheel barrel blindfolded and made it to the other side, everyone was cheering as he took the blindfold off and the preacher came up to shake his hand and hug him, the man said "now preacher do you believe? Yes" the preacher replied, "I do believe I seen It with my own eyes, no" the man said, "do you really believe?" "yes" the preacher said again" I saw it, If you truly believe, then get Into the wheel barrel and we will both go back across." It's one thing to believe in something the secret number seven is to be able to move a mountain with just the faith of a mustard seed. now there are people out there who are Atheist, We all know thru common sense that there are certain animals, birds and fish that are called scavengers, even some atheist who do not believe in any God or Goddess understand that certain foods have a Bacteria that to eat it you have to cook it to a certain temperature to kill this Bacteria, Does this dead bacteria just disappear? does it just go away? no, It is still there, Hopefully it is dead but if you eat this scavenger food and this dead bacteria it is still going thru your stomach, intestines, colon and thru your blood stream so now you understand why some people get some diseases. I want to share with you a true story that is very Important. A woman ate some pork that was not cooked all the way thru, this bacteria went thru her arteries and veins and some wound up in her brain, the bacteria started growing in her brain and became a tumor the size of a big golf ball, she went to the doctor because she was having fainting spells where she would black out, they did some test and scans and found the tumor in her brain. They had to shave her hair off, Cut a big hole in her skull. Remove the tumor then she had to go thru chemotherapy because of

the chance of it being cancerous. This woman
had to go thru all of this ordeal all because she
went to a fast-food restaurant and ate pork. Why
do they call it a fast-food restaurant? Because
they fix the food fast. That is enough on that
matter I want to talk about one of my dreams I
had, It was kind of like the movie Back to the
Future were a silver DeLorean takes off in the air
and time travels into the future or past. there were
several H.G.Wells movies about time machines
so it's cool and maybe that was in my sub-
conscious but in my dream, I was asleep. The
alarm clock woke me up and I took a shower,
shaved, ate breakfast, went to work like I usually
do. I pushed the garage door opener to see It
was raining and thundering and I was driving my
old red Volkswagen bug i had 30 years ago. I
backed out of the driveway and started down the
street, The bug took off in the air and I time
traveled in the past. I wound up in the desert right
before Jesus was crucified. I spent six years
there I could not figure how to get back I married
a widow woman who already Had two boys and
we had another son and another daughter. Could
I have lived during this past lifetime? Was my
fingerprint the same fingerprint I have today?
Then one night I went to sleep, as Usual. I woke
up the next morning to the Sound of the Alarm
clock waking me Up, startled I jumped out of bed
Looked at my watch and the day and realized
during this 8 Hours of sleep I lived six Years of
my Life, I could tell You In great Detail all the
Little things I done each day ,My children's name,
the sheep I was taking care of, My wife of six
years going thru the birth of each baby and not
Having a hospital to take her to and seeing my
baby boy and baby girl being born and watching
them crawl on the floor and learning how to walk.
How can I remember six years in one 8-hour
night? in this other world, Time does not mean
anything, a day is as a Thousand years i
remember reading that somewhere in the Bible,
so the dinosaurs could be living for millions of
years and that would be just like a month or two,

did these cave man have fingerprints also? Are we the only civilization that has a fingerprint? When I woke up and I realized it was only eight hours gone by and I knew I had to go to work so I took my shower, ate my breakfast and pushed open the garage door opener to find it was thundering and raining. I hopped in my red VW bug and backed out of the driveway and paused. do I want to put this in forward and take a chance on going back in time? It was pouring down rain I put it in gear and drove back into the garage and closed the garage door opener I called in sick and went back to bed. I had some sick time built up and I did not want to take a chance going into the past and spending six years, Yes It was fun, learning a new language trying to learn a new custom, marrying a beautiful woman and having two beautiful children, could that be me from a past life? What happened? Did I get killed? How could I have lived six years in one 8-hour period? I Thought about writing a book about my ordeal but realized there are so many other books about people who have time traveled in the past or In the future and their world was a lot more exciting so probably no one would read it they would Think I just imagined it and had a dream from my sub-conscious imagination. Or another what if? If you have read this much of this book, immortality, and have read any other of my books you will see i say the same thing over and over in various books, why? How do you remember something? Only thru repetitions, right? They are ready, the microphone is attached to my shirt, on with the show: "first I want to talk a little about Paul, most of His writings were around 60-70 ad which was thirty years after the death of Christ and remember the ruler of this world is the first-born Son of our God and Goddess and that is Satan, Is he a Angel or Demon? According to Moses when he was talking to Eve, He was a very handsome Angel, then God turned Him into a snake, right? When Paul was on the road to Damascus a bright light blinded him for three days and this bright light told him, its ok to eat

scavenger foods and do whatever you want to
you are No Longer under the Law. So, do You
Worship God or Paul? A lot of people teach
Paul's writings, and This is what He did Write,
now the question could this be the Same Angel
Who told Eve it was ok to eat the forbidden
apple? We know Satan has Been around he
wants you to be scattered and confused Jesus
talked about "Beware of wolves in sheep clothing
they will fool even the Elect" our God went to a lot
of trouble In Leviticus to teach us that some foods
are considered clean while other foods are
considered unclean or scavenger foods, It's the
same with the true 7th day Saturday Sabbath this
is a Commandment, actually number four that
has more word, more detail, than any of the other
Commandments and we know Constantine in
313ad Did Change the Original 7th day Saturday
Sabbath to the 1st day of the Week Sunday this
started the Roman Catholic Church. they wanted
to keep the Goddess, so they had to hide her as
the Virgin Mary and still do worship the Goddess
that way. The point is I asked God a long time
ago to give me This "Understanding Heart" Read
1Kings chapter 3 If You ask God in prayer for this
understanding heart then be ready for a lot of
questions I still Ask a Lot of Questions, You have
the right to ask questions and demand answers
That is Why It's so Important for Wiccall to Grow
and It will only with your help, I promise Goddess
I would put Her back to where She was, It's up to
you, the reader to finish this." End of Chapter 12

Chapter 13 episode 13

The old man is in his living room relaxing in his
recliner, drink in hand as the camera zooms in
the old man speaks. "A lot of people think the
number 13 is bad luck. If you look at the original
12 Disciples following our Jesus Christ, then
Jesus would be the 13th person walking around
in the group. You go to some hotels and big
buildings they eliminate the 13th floor. it's simply
called the 14th floor. We already talked about the
story you can give a person a fish and feed them

for a day or you can teach that person to fish and feed them for a lifetime. that works for anything, all we know is what we were taught or not taught. Would it be cool to have a Fishermen church ministry in every town? A non-denominational church that never passes the offering plate around. Yes, it does take a lot of money to run a church ministry so the offering box is at the door as you go in or go out it also says Tithes, offerings and prayer request so what you give is between you and your creator would Jesus come to this church? Only if you were there on the 7th day Saturday sabbath. I do not see my Jesus going to a so-called Fishermen church on Sunday, the 1st day of the week or eating scavenger food. What if you are not saved by grace? What if Jesus did not die for your sins? most Christians were taught that you are saved by Grace, all you have to do is say the three magic words, God forgive me, and you get to go to a Heaven forever and ever or if you do not, then you will burn in a fiery hell forever and ever, it's not your fault, this is what you were Taught this is how a few control you. What if they were taught wrong? It's not your fault.   Another problem is you were probably taught as a Christian that Jesus Christ died for your sins but that is wrong too. Jesus was allowed to die to do away with the animal sacrificial law only. Why should an innocent animal die for something you did? Remember when Jesus was alive there was no Welfare, no Section 8 housing and no food stamps, so how do we take care of the crippled, disease, handicap and poor people? The Jewish people came up with this scam to get people to atone for their sins to bring them a sacrificial Animal and they would pray over it and feed the poor, but the Jewish got very rich off of this scam and did not want this Jesus Christ to show the world their scam, so they had to kill Jesus to silence him. You can no longer grab a innocent animal and take it to a Rabbi and expect all your sins to be forgiven, you are accountable, that is why there is Re-Incarnation, each life you get to

live so many years and yes you do die and are
Judged and go into another Re-Incarnated body
according to your sins, now you understand
Immortality you are an immortal spirit soul, you
have lived many lifetimes, You see a child born
crippled, disease, handicap, poor or mental
problems and you wonder why? Maybe the sins
of a past life? Can you imagine a baby being
born in a hospital bed, breathing, eating and
drinking thru his mother's umbilical cord, then a
nurse spanks the baby on their feet, the baby lets
out their last mother breath, then as the baby
inhales a new, Immortal spirit soul enters the
baby, did the spirit show up as a black smoke,
like in the movies? Did the baby's eyes turn a
glossy black like in the movies to show you the
spirit, entered it? What if the spirit soul was a
good person? Could the smoke be white, and the
baby's eyes turn a pretty blue or emerald, green
for a second? Now the spirit soul is alive again,
eating what the baby eats, drinking what the baby
drinks, experiencing what that baby is
experiencing, the spirit soul wants to talk and tell
the world what is going on but can only cry or
mutter, maybe now a different skin color, different
hair color, different eye color, learn a different
language, different religion, learn a new job, you
see hospitals like St. Jude that takes care of little
babies, born crippled, blind, handicap, some
disease or illness, what about being born with no
fingerprint? No hands, no arms, is that baby
going thru his or her hell right now? Is our God
merciful enough, instead of burning in a fiery hell
forever and be this is a little bit better? Now you
grow up again and again, each time learn a new
experience in a new mortal, flesh and blood
temporary body with a immortal spirit soul
learning, experiencing new things? Think about it,
let's change the subject, how about another
motivational story? We realize there are million,
billion, trillion different people all on their own
path, all doing what they need to do to
Experience what they need to do during this
lifetime and each person having to do what they

need to do to experience all the different things they want to do and then something happens. Some drunk runs a red light and crashes in your car and accidently kills you. Did you get to experience all the things you wanted to do during this lifetime? No, why? Some drunk ran a red light and killed me. So now your physical flesh and blood body is dead, and your Spirit/ Soul is judged it's not your fault you still got a lot of things you wanted to do but life is a bitch then you die, so now what happens? Do you have to start all over go into a womb and spend 9 months upside down surrounded by water then come out kicking and screaming and learn how to talk, maybe a different language, different culture different religion? walk and go thru learning the ABC of life. Can you just go to the school and say give me my high school diploma? No, you have to go thru your 12 years maybe you can skip a year or better off you may be allowed to attach yourself to another flesh and blood human who is trying to do similar things to what you were doing. This is what we call a split personality a Spirit/Soul attaches to another Spirit/Soul, kind of like a Jekyll and Hyde but sometimes one is not good, and one is not evil so can we have a person with a split personality? Can we have a person with multiple personality? Can these be entities that did not get the chance to Experience all the things they wanted to Experience, and their particular life was shortened due to a freak accident? Can there really be freak accidents? Is everything in life pre-ordained? Can that guy who was drunk run the red light because that is what he needed to Experience? maybe He needed to Experience going to Jail, going to court, being sued and go thru the humiliation of knowing your drunken attitude killed a family, and changed their life and now It's changing your life. How many people are now affected because of one simple ordeal? New day new act new scene new clothes new glass of Dr.pepper, cold drink in hand relaxing on my sofa." Now another story it was about two normal high school kids who came from about the same type family after they graduated one got married had children and got a typical job, The other became very wealthy they had a ten year re-union. They talked about all the wild crazy things they done then the one asked what happened how come you are so rich, and I am just getting by? The rich friend said come over tomorrow to my house, He gave him his address and we will go swimming and I will tell you the secret. Excited he went home and told his wife and kids so the next day He was amazed to see the address was one of the biggest ocean front properties In the town. He pulled up in the circular drive, was greeted by the guard who escorted Him to the Front door, There the butler escorted him to the main living room and said, "he will be down to see you in a moment" The rich friend came down the stairs wearing a bathing suit and towel, "ready to go". He looked at his friend and said, "I thought I told you we were going swimming?" " Yes", the poor friend replied," I forgot all about that I wanted to know your secret just tell me", The rich friend replied" It does not work like that, We have to go swimming first", he calls his butler to bring a extra bathing suit and spare towel he goes In the guest bathroom and changes They walk around, him showing everything and they go outside to the ocean the rich friend grabs a life saver jacket out of the pile and says" Let's go swimming", The poor friend looks at the pile and thinks he is a good swimmer and He does not need a Life Jacket so they Jump in and swim around, the poor friend said" I thought you were going to tell me your secret" the rich friend swam way out in the water and said "come out here I do not want anyone to hear", The water was way over His head but he was a good swimmer. "first", The rich friend said. "You have to listen to what others say. I told you we were going swimming, you were not prepared, so you failed lesson one" " Ok" the poor friend said, " I am sorry but now what?". The rich friend went on "second Lesson I grabbed a life saver jacket, you did not, again you

do not come prepared, now the water is over your
head, and you cannot stay out here very long,
you have eyes, but you do not see, you have ears
but do not hear" " ok" he said " I will learn, please
tell me the secret". Then the rich friend pushed
him under water and held him there a few
moments, coming up for air gasping saying,
"What are you trying to do? drown me?" The rich
friend replied, "at that moment you were under
water what did you want more than anything
more than all the money, mansions, fancy cars
etc.?" " I wanted to breath" "Yes" he replied
"When you want to succeed as much as you want
to breath then and only then will you succeed" "I
found by talking to people what they wanted and
needed, Everything In business is all about
supply and demand. If someone demands
something then someone else will supply that
need, its simple. You can have the best donut
shop in the world but If there are already five
donut shops in the area then you may not
succeed. People will not drive 20 miles to get
your donut so It has to be for a local area, It's all
about location and supply and demand, be
prepared, look the person in the eye, That is
something you rarely ever do why?" " I don't know
I guess i am shy you know me I always have
been that way". "Yes, that is part of your down-
fall, my grandpa gave me some good advice a
long time ago, look the person in the eye, tell
them what you will do, give a firm handshake and
keep your promise a man, or woman Is only as
good as their word. That is the secret" now listen
to another story there may be a secret there also
they got back to shore and layed out on the
beach enjoying each other's company and the
warmth of the sun.". I remember about nine
years ago after we graduated, I was a wild and
crazy person I had long hair and a beard plus all
the bad ass tattoos to show my rebellion. The
problem was society judges you by what you look
like. It was hard for me to find a decent job, one
day out of frustration I went into the bathroom,
Looked in the mirror and I did not like what I

seen, I shaved my beard off and cut some of my hair, when I walked out of that bathroom, my dog started barking at me, he did not recognize me, even my little kids when I reached down to pick them up ,they looked at me and started crying i had to hold them and assure them it's still the same me Inside it took a Little while to get used to the new me and even doubting Thomas who knew the real Jesus Christ did not recognize Him we all know the story so Jesus had to flee the town. Was Jesus actually married? Yes, Mary of Magdalene was his wife. Did he actually Have Children? Yes, two boys and One girl It was a law to be a Rabbi you had to be married upstanding in your community and have a male son to keep the bloodline going. everyone knew Jesus was a Rabbi, he carried the credentials, maybe the breastplate or some way people could identify he was a Jewish Rabbi himself. did they all have fingerprints? Yes, are their DNA still out there? Yes, the children's grandchildren all the way down the blood line of Jesus Christ is still out there. The movie called the Da Vinci code talks a lot of this where did they get these ideas from? They searched for the truth, there are spirit entities out there today just like there was spirit entities back then. We all have our Guardian Angel watching over us and sometimes we want to Ignore what they are trying to Teach us so sometimes we need to go back into the womb, Learn a new language, Learn a new custom and learn a new culture so can you do all the things you want to experience in one life-time? no, one of my secret's Is the fact the real Jesus Christ did teach reincarnation, This is immortality 101 you are living it, There are no pearly gates, no streets of gold and no mansions, You are in your heaven/hell right now, you are not saved by grace but are accountable this is where Avalon Fishermen church ministry will fit in, once you understand there is a female side of God and we all have one religion inside of us yes, we can still be different, speak a different language and culture and customs. You have to decide, all you

know is what you were taught. your sub-
conscious will only accept what you tell it to
believe in, you be the judge, at least think about
what we are saying I am either right or wrong.
What part of what we are saying is right? What
part of what We are saying is wrong? Who gets to
decide if we are right? Who gets to decide If we
are wrong?" Now my friend I do Have to go back
to work, It was great seeing you again maybe we
can get together hope you think about my secret I
will help you get established You have to decide
what you want to do, End of chapter 13

Chapter 14 episode 14

The old man is speaking again "just Imagine if
you had all the money in the world, what would
you do? Sure, it would be fun setting around
counting all the money, but after a while you
would want to do something, maybe help others I
want to build custom built environmental quality
homes, completely off the grid with our own
power, solar, windmill and water treatment plants
etc. I just became a good motivational speaker
instead maybe you can help me get this general
contractor development project off the ground
what do you think?" "Yes " he replied, "I am very
interested" "Then think about it and I will get back
with you see you later"   I hope this will be the
last book I wrote. I said that last time thinking we
said all I needed to say, then I have these crazy
dreams and the spirit tells me more stuff. In my
dream world if I am seeing, hearing and touching
things then did I leave my fingerprint there? I
know I asked this before, but I want you to think
about this millions, billions, trillions of different
people thru out the world in this lifetime so
imagine the last two three thousand years how
many different people all here for a different
reason going down a different path why? Where
are you going? Where have you been? Have you
experience everything you want to? Did you leave
your fingerprint there? People talk about the
tombstone they want on their grave site they put
their name, the date they were born and the date

they died, sometimes the only thing between these two dates is the dash, people say what is your dash? What did you accomplish during this lifetime? Did you leave your fingerprint? When you stand before this creator on your judgement day, how will he recognize you from the million, billion, trillion others out there? He created this fingerprint; He knows the hair on your head. You see people in every life going thru disease, sickness, cancer, handicap, rich, poor, all walks of life, all cultures, all languages, some because they did some bad things in their previous life, others because they chose to experience these things. what do you need to experience? This lifetime I learned a little about patience and perseverance, i was always in a hurry, why? I wanted to accomplish so much in a short time. Now I am more relaxed, if I do not get to see the seven wonders in this lifetime then I will make it a priority to add it to my bucket list in my next lifetime." next act next scene everyone is ready the old man speaks: "another story or what you want to call a secret talks about a crazy Man in a Insane asylum, the nurse asked him what he would like for Christmas and he said, I want a wheel barrel, What on earth would you do with a wheel barrel, she said laughing? I Would go around and ask everyone's problems and put all their problems in the wheel barrel, so all the nurses chipped in and bought him a shiny new red wheel barrel. One day the nurse came to work to see the guy dragging the wheel barrel upside down, she walked up to him and asked what happened, He said I went to everybody and asked them all their problems and the wheel barrel got so heavy I could not push it anymore. She thought for a moment and said, "what If you get an imaginary shovel and dig a imaginary hole and bury all these people's problems?" Smiling he said that would work. So, we all have excess baggage and sometimes we need to put all our problems in a imaginary wheel barrel and dig a imaginary hole with a imaginary shovel and put all our problems in the hole, bury them and forget were we buried them. But our male chauvinistic attitude that we are man with big balls and testosterone, so we are the rulers, Is it our ego? our pride? our vanity? 2,000 years later have we, as a society and as different cultures learned anything." I feel the presence of the ghost camera "she is still here, constantly filming my every move, yes even when I go to the bathroom, I feel her presence. I realize she Is my guardian angel sent to constantly watch over me. she is filming everything to document before our creators everything. Remember when someone told you they felt their whole life flash before you at that moment? This is actually what is happening. I read this book called wisdoms and the first wisdom was called Duality ,the symbol for duality is a coin showing there are two sides to everything, good and evil, left and right, up and down, forward and reverse so If you look at your life you can use that Wisdom to make you a better person you now realize you do have good and evil Inside of you It's a percentage just like If you are a male during this life then you would have the male hormone Testosterone Inside of you, but you would also have all little of the female hormone called Estrogen Inside you also. Scientist and Doctors have proven this. I would Like to think of when I was young and the schoolteacher was trying to teach us fractions, she would draw this big circle on the board and say this is a big pie so If you cut this big pie In half then you half this Line drawn thru the middle showing now you have two halves of a pie, so two halves equal a whole. This is simple teaching that a child had to learn. they both had the male hormone testosterone and estrogen Inside of them. Now I want to talk a moment of these hormones. A long time ago when I was In the Baptist, Christian religion I was taught that being Gay or a Lesbian was a Sin, a terrible Abomination against the Bible teaching. everyone has read the Bible story about Sodom and Gomorrah. I was taught If you go to a bathroom, pull your clothes off and look down and you see a male penis then you need to act like a man, that is what you are during this particular lifetime. Now we have the hormones we can add if needed but this is only the physical side of us, everyone knows there are three sides to every Individual, physical, mental and spiritual. I can see how some people maybe a female in a past life and having a total recall of that person and carrying over some of these emotions, feelings and baggage. I know a Lot of gay people who tell me they are a woman trapped in this man's body. Changing your hormone by adding the steroid testosterone will help physically but mentally they still believe they are still a woman. We know the female has the same problem thinking they are a male trapped in this woman's body again now you are a female in this life, Get some estrogen, forget your past life, Enjoy being a female in this life and experience what you need to experience as a female, maybe in your next life you get to be a male or whatever you want but do not play God and look down and not be happy with what you are today. God does not make mistakes God made you a female or a male for a reason you need to experience these and not create some diseases because mentally you remember what you are in a past life forget all the past life drama, you are a male now act like a male, you are a female now, act like a female. physically add hormones, mentally Seek counseling spiritually Be the person God/ Goddess created enjoy each Life to the fullest. Why are you a male in one life and a female in another life anyway? Why can't you just be the same life after life? Then how do You experience different things if you are a cookie cutter life after life would the world be pretty boring If you knew exactly what you are going to do in each life after life after life? Being gay or a lesbian is not a new thing, our societies and different cultures have been dealing with this situation since the beginning. What is the answer? Just like a pack of wolves they have an alpha Wolf or alpha dog which is the biggest, baddest, meanest dog, is the alpha dog and that

is the leader, so goliath was obvious the alpha
dog, right? Sometimes in our society, our culture
we have a alpha Dog as our leader He needs to
be the biggest, baddest, meanest person around
and He gets to be the king, right? You have to
obey the king; He can't be some whiney wimpy
kid ruling a great nation but that was what David
was. He picked up a little rock and hit goliath in
the only vulnerable spot right between the eyes.
all of his armor did him no good, everyone has
their Achilles heel their vulnerable spot. What is
your weak-ness? Lucifer knows. He is the god of
this world. He Is the first-born son of this God and
Goddess, yes Jesus was a important person. Just
like Hercules was born half man half God so too
was Jesus born half male and half God to do
away with this sacrificial law and to teach you the
truth. Duality teaches the wisdom that Inside us If
you take that pie and cut it in half then cut each
half into half then you have one fourth times four
so Inside of you now, you have this duality of
good as being three fourths and evil as only one
fourth. If You are created during this lifetime as a
male species, then you have three fourth make
hormone called testosterone and one fourth
hormone called estrogen Inside of you. This is
normal. You cannot go to a doctor or surgeon and
tell him to use this fancy laser surgery and
remove this evil out of you or remove this female
hormone out of you. It cannot happen. We have
figured this hormone thing out and now we can
take a hormone substitute and change our
balance which is what some weightlifters and
body builders do so they are changing their
hormone balance with steroids, and we do not
know what the long term affect will be. We also
found this hormone called human growth
hormone and we figured out we can put this into
our cattle, chickens and other food supply to
make them stronger and better and now we are
eating this and changing our hormone levels you
can see 12 year old girls developing breast and
young boys being developed before their time we
do not know the long term effect on this will be we

are playing God and creating sperm and egg thru Artificial Insemination and we will eventually think we are a god of some kind. Lucifer and all his cohorts are just setting back laughing their butts off at the silly humans trying to be gods. We steal from the mother earth, dig holes in Her and steal her diamonds, emerald, gold, silver, oil and gas and think It belongs to you. We do not realize we came into this world naked and with nothing and we will leave this world naked and with nothing all the material things we think we own will not buy us a extra moment here on this earth. We see tornados, earthquakes tsunami, lightning, rain, thunderstorms, hurricanes etc. next act next scene " I remember when I was a kid, we had this gravel pit close to our home so all the kids would go over there on weekends when everyone were off work and climb on top of the sand pile. Once you climbed on top you could see all over the neighborhood. Things looked different when you are on top of the mountain. As a kid full of energy, you would holler out loud I am the king of this mountain, and you would dare anyone to take it from you. Of course, It depends on how many other kids were there and they would climb up the mountain, but you had the advantage, you were already up there so It was easy to push them back down The only rule was once you fell down with either knee touching the ground you had to give up for that day, now tomorrow you could come back and challenge again. I got to stay up on top of the mountain for a while eventually I got tired and after wrestling with three guys the fourth one who came up grabbed my legs, surprised at the new maneuver I was off balance. Now I know the basic karate stanch and that is balance one foot in front the other Foot behind at an angle to keep you balanced but after a while your energy will go out, so I tumbled down the mountain along with my pride. Now I want to talk about good and evil Inside of you which one Is the strongest? The one you feed the most. If you feed evil, then you become evil, if you feed good then you become good, it's not rocket science its normal everyday living life 101 enjoy this life be somebody. It's not just martin Luther king who said it, but you too can say it. I am somebody, I may not be rich but i am somebody. I may be black, white, brown or yellow, but I am somebody. God and the Goddess created you in their image in the image of us you have a unique fingerprint no one else has that so yes you are somebody. Are you ready to become the 13th warrior? Immortality cowboy church ministry needs warriors all over the world, in every city every town to help teach society the truths. is this the truth? What part of what I am saying is true? What part of what I am saying not true? All you know is what you were taught, your sub-conscious will only accept what you tell it to believe in, they can only teach you what they were taught, and their sub-conscious will only accept what they tell it to believe in who Is right? Who Is wrong Who gets to decide? So, what does all these motivational stories have to do with the immortality cowboy Ministry? I want the world to know that this is not just a Christian Ministry It is a worldwide non-denominational ministry to teach the real Jesus Christ. Does this cowboy church have to be a physical church you go to once or twice a week? Can the immortality cowboy church be a way of life, not just physical but also mentally and spiritually? Now you understand who you are, why you are here, where are you going do you need a physical church with wood and brick to prove this? No so does that mean if Lucifer Is the real first-born son of our God and Goddess then is our Jesus Christ brothers? Yes, even Lucifer took Jesus up on the mountain and did all kinds of tests and what happened? Lucifer took him back down and admitted "Surely this is the son of God so yes they are brothers. Lucifer was kicked out of heaven, but he is still the only power to be the Holy Spirit. if you have read this and want to help Build a Avalon church ministry in your area Let me know I can help you set It up. What would the world be like If we had a Immortality cowboy church ministry In every town, every city, every state and all over the world? Would the world be a better place if millions of people read my books and understood these principles? Not because I wrote them, I am no body, just a crazy rebel teacher Trying to teach people his version of the truth. Now you know all the elusive treasures without rubbing the Aladdin lamp, but do you get the one wish? Do you now have this Understanding heart? "Yes, I am immortal, this book Is all about immortality, It Is up to you to wake up and realize maybe you to have an immortal Spirit/Soul. Is grandma up in heaven with Jesus Christ right now or is she still in the ground waiting on this future rapture to come? neither. She has lived this life, she has experienced what she needed to experience, yes, her temporary flesh and blood mortal body did die and yes, she was your grandmother during this lifetime, she needed to experience being a grandmother and you needed to experience her as your grandmother. She has been judged and probably in another life. now you understand why some people go thru a life with certain disease's, certain illness or handicap, blind, etc. You cannot experience everything you need to experience in only one lifetime. It's impossible to experience everything you need to experience in a hundred lifetimes you have a right to ask questions and demand answers. You are here to experience you could have an immortal spirit/soul only you can answer that question tell all your friends the elusive treasure's They are to be shared they are free; you paid the price of the book, so let others read it, originally, I wrote this book with five secrets being of a religious nature and I used only five of these you are currently reading. If you go to Amazon books and type in my name, Melvin Abercrombie You will see most of my books are of a religious nature. To me, the world is not following five Laws. I wanted to finally make a book with a Goddess, Re-incarnation, the Kosher Food law, keeping the True 7th day Saturday sabbath and you are not saved by Grace but then I wanted to add the story about the messiah so If

you add all this to call this Olde Religion Wiccal
then you can understand were all this is going I
am not creating a new religion I am not the Anti-
Christ ,I love Jesus Christ He is my Lord and
Savior I accept his teachings. Why did the Church
kill him? They knew He was telling many secrets;
I like to call them elusive treasure's and they had
to kill him to silence Him, now over 2,000 Years
later we are still scattered and confused
Whatever name you want to call the Worship of a
male God and a female Goddess as equal is up
to you. I choose Yahweh and Shekhinah and to
use the name Avalon Fishermen Church ministry
as the missing Holy Grail, we want to think of a
fishermen type nondenominational church
ministry, and you can use this name in your area.
Let me know I can help you set it up. This would
be the one Church that our God, Yahweh would
approve of and our one Goddess, Shekhinah
approve of. Now would Jesus Christ feel
comfortable in a fishermen's type Church. Yes, I
cannot picture my Jesus Christ with a cowboy hat
and boots, but then on the other hand I cannot
picture my Jesus Christ in a suit and tie either. If
Jesus Christ walked into an Avalon Fishermen
church on Saturday, the 7th day of the week and
was called a fishermen type church then Yes, I
feel my Jesus would go there and give His
blessings, time will tell. The Olde World Order or
a New World Order. only with equality will we
ever have harmony and balance, United we stand
divided we fall. Lucifer wants you to be scattered
and confused. He Is doing everything in his
power to block you from reading this" Can we add
more cool stories? it's up to the producers and
directors we are at the movie studio we see a lot
of camera and stage scenes.   setting in a chair
Melvin Abercrombie speaks" this book is all
about what happens after the Movie, the
Interview, was Brigette Monroe a real person?
can she be the imaginary, fictional, make believe,
granddaughter of Marilyn Monroe? what happens
now? Did our Jesus actually die on the cross and
is in heaven right now? Last we saw was Jesus

walking away from the town to flee from being nailed to a cross again. some churches and religions want you to believe he just went up to heaven with God the father forever and ever and left and abandoned his wife and children? Did the world change because Jesus was born? We know something very dramatic had to happen to change the world from a B.C. Time to a A.D. time We want to think of our God the Father as a Old, long gray hair and a beard so is our God Old? we see pictures and statues of little Angels we call these baby Angels Cherubs, again, do they grow up and go thru their terrible two's and learn to crawl, walk, talk and eventually become teenager angels going thru their hormone problem at the age of thirteen? do they grow up to be young adult angels and then get married and eventually die thousands of years later? So did God the Father and Goddess, the mother die? Is the Goddess actually a Vampire? We want to scare our children by creating another blood sucking monster, we are all either Carnivorous or vegetarian, do you eat meat? Some people like their steaks rare, some actually like blood pudding and rare meat, If you get hungry enough you will become a cannibal, we know thru out history different tribes do that, are they all demonic/ What was demonic a thousand years ago is different than today. We want to label and judge people who believe different then we do. could this be why the time changed. Is Lucifer now a creator of this new world order where there is only a male God and yes, we will eventually evolve thru evolution to a one language, one people, one religion and one church entity worshipping this one male Dominant God forever and ever? Yes, in a past life or several past lives I used the name Merlyne as my name, thru the years I got to go into a lot of different type flesh and blood human mortal bodies and get to experience some of the cool things most I remember a fondness of mother earth and mother nature I would rather be outside then stuck in a house or home, I felt relaxed and at

ease touching our Earth. I feel like a cowboy
church is not just a one day a week Church
Meeting place but a lifestyle of every day. Can we
make this world, our world a better place to live?
Can we, as one person do anything to help make
this world a better place? Can we help others by
teaching and showing them that we have a
beautiful world here? Can we get some useless
bottom land that no one wants and get bulldozers
and backhoes and clear it out, move the dirt
around dig a big pond and use that dirt to build up
the other part, cut down all the brush and recycle
the wood shavings, create water front housing
property with our own energy from solar panels
and windmills, create our own water treatment
plant and aerobic water septic system so we do
not add to the sewer problems, build roads and
sidewalks and some commercial property with a
dollar store and grocery store. Now have a Tax
base the city can get some money back on
property taxes and make the area a better place
by turning some useless bottom land into
something nice. Why does no one do this?
because they cannot make any money, it's all
about the mighty dollar. If you are a part of the
church as Avalon development company then
you are not a for profit company, yes you pay
your share of taxes like everyone else does but
you do not want to make a profit. You want to hire
good people, pay them a fair salary for a fair
amount of work you create your own concrete
company so you can pour your own concrete and
have your own nonprofit company to bull doze
and create a large lake so when it does rain all
the water will go there and the rest of the useless
bottom land now becomes waterfront property.
what would it be like if we did this in every city?
does every city have some useless bottom land
that no one wants? Can we clear it out enough to
build a large lake make it twenty or thirty feet
deep, take the dirt out and spread around to the
other land and when it rains the water will go to
where we want it yes it takes money to build a
church. We need a lot of people who will give ten

percent of their money to what they believe in, again we will never pass an offering plate around those who believe in Avalon will give accordingly. God knows and that is all that matters. are you a fisher of men? Can you teach a person to fish? Can you feed that person for a lifetime? What can you do to make this world a better place? First read this book and tell others every penny that comes from the sale of these books all goes to Avalon church ministry yes would love to have at least one Avalon fishermen church in every town. Do you have one in your town? If not send me a e-mail I will help you get it set up. Would the World be a better place if we had a Avalon Church in every town? Do we actually need a physical wood and brick building you only go to once or twice a week? Avalon is a state of mind you can have 24 7 365 if you want it. we are not creating some new fangle Church. We are going back to the Olde Skool, the Olde Law, The Olde World Order yes there is a Male God and a Female Goddess, yes, we have equality. Yes, Jesus did teach re-Incarnation you have lived many lifetimes admit it or not deep down you know it makes sense ask yourself what would the real Jesus Christ do? Would Jesus eat pork or other scavenger foods? No, he would not, so why do you? Would Jesus keep the true 7th day Saturday sabbath? Yes, it's a part of the Command-ments, number 4 we are under the law Jesus said if you love me keep my commandments .You have this illusion that you are saved by grace you can go out do whatever sin you want to and wait till the last minute and right before you die say the 3 magic words God forgive me and get to go to a heaven forever and ever but does that make sense? Jesus is the Messiah, the ha mashiach, why would God pick joseph knowing he was from the right bloodline of the tribe of Judah, the lion of Judah, knowing that the ha mashiach would have to come from that bloodline then not use him?? I believe thru the years the "versions" of the bible have been changed If the spirit of God did go into joseph and the holy ghost, the wife of God, the Shekhinah, went into the virgin Mary then in the physical world joseph and Mary were legally having sex and the marriage was legal with the bloodline coming down from joseph. in the spiritual world God Yahweh had sex with his wife, Shekhinah and a child was born the son of our God the ha mashiach the Messiah. If joseph was told to not lay with his wife, then they were never married and Jesus is not the Messiah and God broke his own laws of Deuteronomy22, A lot of people did not want this Rabbi Jesus to teach these 8 truths, so they had to Kill him to silence him. The Jewish Rabbi's wanted him dead so bad they were willing to let a known murderer go free to silence Jesus." We stop for a moment take a break then Rex Speaks: "The old man wants us to contact a local Jewish Synagogue and set up a meeting with all the important Jewish Rabbi's. He wants to go into a Jewish chapel and see for himself a typical Jewish church service. He admits he is just a uncircumcised Gentile, unworthy of going into a Jewish Holy of holies and see firsthand the tabernacle, the scrolls ,the torah, the Tanakh, the typical Jewish singing and worship service that his Jesus Christ did go to and hopefully convince these Jewish leaders that his Jesus Christ, the Yeshua Christus is their messiah, their ha mashiach, so imagine going to a typical Jewish church and listening to all the beautiful songs and the ceremony and having all the rabbi and the old man setting at a table talking among themselves, trying to understand who is right and who is wrong. Does this book convince you, the reader that maybe the old man is not just full of horse shit but now maybe some of the things he is saying could be true? Now we have a Avalon Fishermen church and a lifestyle, or do we? It's up to you, read this book, share with others or keep going to a false church on Sunday and hope you get to go to a heaven forever and ever." rex pauses and in walks jasmine, she says "ok cowboy you have said enough, now it is my turn" smiling rex tips his hat and walks away, the

camera turns to jasmine: " You know I was born
in Japan my ancestors were the samurai warriors,
I was trained in karate, judo and various other
self-defense and was taught our God of our
family was buddha. I had no choice the first 14
years of my life this was what I was taught. then I
realized there were other people out there who
worshipped a different type of God or a female as
a Goddess, this fascinated me as a equal. I came
to America went to the Police academy and
Joined the FBI for five years found out the old
man was interested in me as an addition to his
personal Body guard staff, I checked him out and
realized it's not about the money, I read some of
His books and wanted to be a part of this family, I
wanted to know if there is another God beside my
buddha then who was he? Never in my lifetime
would I believe I could ever fall in love with Rex
and these teachings of the old man, now made
sense to me. So, can we add more scenes of
different other Angels coming here and talking?
Let people know who they really are and kind of
what they could look like during this lifetime? If
we all die, then do they all die too? Again, we see
baby angels and we call them Cherubs so do
they grow up to be teenage angel's and young
adult angels? do they ever get married and have
little bambino baby angels? If our God and
Goddess gave us this power to create so does
our God and Goddess allow the Angels to do the
same? This has been a great Mini-series I want
to think the movie producers, directors, all the
camera people all the cool special effects and
behind the scenes people who made this into a
movie, this is not fiction this is reality. There is a
male God and a female Goddess they are alive.
You can put your blinders on and say there is no
spirit world, and you can call yourself an atheist
or an evolutionist. Actually, I believe in evolution
to a point. I see pictures of me when I was a baby
and a kid, then as a teenager and young adult so
I know I have evolved thru the years so evolution
has happened in my and your life that is obvious.
I do not believe that fish just came out of the

water and sprouted hands and legs and evolved into humans if that was so then we would still see it happening. There has to be a higher power of something in another world or Dimension that did create us. We can say yes, they are UFO or aliens from another planet. What gives us the right to say we are the only planet that has life? This book is about all the rebel angels and rebel Church's out there. Originally The Romans, Greeks, Egyptians and many other cultures did believe in equality. They not only Worshipped a Male type of God but a female Type Goddess, they just called them by different names where they rebels? Where they part of the original Brotherhood?   One male ruler over millions of people but is it kind of like our one male president over millions of people? are we that much different today? A time will come, and we will eventually have a female as our president that almost happened with Hillary. So, is this inevitable? are we going back to this equality? The world is slowly evolving into a new, one race of people when black and white inter-marry and have half black, half white children. This is also going on with the spanish and oriental and now more than other, the gay and lesbian people are standing up for equality, so can we imagine a couple hundred years from now there not being a Caucasian race or an African American race? or even a Hispanic or an oriental race? we know in the beginning, we all spoke one language so Adam, eve and all their children probably spoke the Hebrew tongue. These were not the circumcised Jewish people who took over the race, but the universal language of today is the English language. you can go to any country, and it is to their best interest to learn the English language so would it be safe to say there will be a time in the future were English is the chosen language and one race of people will evolve again? I have seen a black man and a white woman have a baby and it is beautiful, but do we call this child a Caucasian or an African American? Same with white and Spanish, the children turn out beautiful and the white and oriental children again makes beautiful children, we see these children growing up in our society and we can tell they are half breeds. Like it or not we are slowly evolving into this new world order." Jasmine stops speaking the camera goes to the old man's bedroom he is setting in his chair having a drink as the camera zooms in the old man speaks:" my mother's side of the family, my grandfather was Irish and my grandmother was Cherokee Indian, so my mother was a half breed and I am a mixed breed myself. You can still see the freckles from my Irish side and then my dad's side of the family grandpa Thomas Jefferson Abercrombie was I thought German but under Ancestry.com the Abercrombie name is Scottish, so my heritage is it Celtic?   Is it Teutonic or Cherokee? Can I be a warlock and a psychic vampyre at the same time? Can I worship a male God and a female Goddess as equal? Can I teach the real Jesus Christ as part of this warlock brotherhood? If I use the word brotherhood can that include our sisters and the female race of people? We no longer have a pure Aryan race of people or if we do, they are in a minority. Did our God and Goddess let us go to this extreme and standby and watch and see what we would do then slowly bring us back to a one world religion with a one world people but is this a part of this new world government some are trying to create? Is there just good and evil and that is it? can we have a hundred shades of gray or 666 shades of red which is another book i wrote along the same lines. If you ever want to get a hold of me, I have nothing to hide I will open debate with any preacher or anyone, bring your "version" of your holy bible and what you think actually did happen you can mail me a letter, send me an e-mail I will talk as brothers and sisters we all do not know everything. but everything I have taught is true as far as I can tell, prove me wrong. I will apologize. If I am right, will you help out? you have the right to ask questions and demand answers, I hope you were brave enough to read this entire book,

very few will. I hope it did wake you up a little,
yes, a lot of these stories are in my other books
also why? Again, I have to have so many pages
to make a book, sure I can write a book with four
or five hundred pages but if you want to make this
into a movie then someone will have to delete so
many words and stories, this way this book will be
less than 100 pages and can be put into a two-
hour movie or a lot of one hour miniseries, every
week. Can you add more stories from different
books? sure I wrote over a hundred books
screenplays all at amazon, Barnes and noble,
books a million and eBay under my name, Melvin
Abercrombie, go ahead and check me out.
Remember most of my books to write them I had
to have so many pages for them to accept them
so I had a great idea then had to put the same
stories over and over again to make into a book
so if you read a lot of my books, you will see I say
the same thing over and over again. This is how
you remember things thru repetition. Can you
look in a mirror and see a little of a rebel angel in
you? Are you brave enough to be a part of the
Brotherhood? To show the world you will wear
the Brotherhood patch on your t shirts, jackets
and other clothing? Would the world be a better
place if we did create more Brotherhood ministry
all over, in every city, every state yes all over the
world? Can we do this without being a rebel
angel? We see a lot of feedback on this new
world order, people are trying to create so is
some energy force talking to them, the same way
they are talking to me and trying to slowly evolve
us all back to a one nation? We dream that one
day we will eventually die and get to go to a
heaven or a hell forever. Can we cry up there?
can there be tears of joy and sadness? We are
taught we will die and are judged, and we go thru
a pearly gate, walk down the street of gold and
everyone gets a mansion, and we live forever and
ever? Is that it? Will we all be one skin color? will
we all speak one language? Will we never grow
old? so how old will we be? Can we eat in
heaven? Can we have a cold glass of iced tea?

Do we go to the bathroom? If we are in a heaven forever and ever, what will we do?" The producers and staff can now show deleted scenes and any other behind the scenes filming showing what all it took to make this into a movie, maybe showing some of the shape-shifting scenes and special effects and what all they had to do to create a scene showing some of the behind-the-scenes people that helped make this into a cool movie. The old man is setting in a recliner a drink in his hand, and he speaks: " I have lived many lifetimes and now they call me a rebel teacher, why? I believe in the Brotherhood and equality, It makes sense there is a male God and a female Goddess, they had a lot of children some were rebellious that is a fact look at our history of all the rebellious church's and rebellious religions still going on. Remember originally there was a roman catholic church and the people who did not like them were called protestors and later became the protestant church which eventually became all the other spin off Christian church's so were these protestors actually rebels? what is the difference between a protestor and a rebel? What is good for you may not be good for someone else again why are you here today? What do you need to experience during this particular lifetime If you do not like a certain church do you have the right to protest or be a rebel and leave that denomination? We have this dream of having one heaven where we can live forever and ever but wake up, that is all it is, another dream. You cannot possibly do everything you want or need to do in only one lifetime. accept it or not form your own rebellion if you do not like the choices out there does this series end? Can we continue with cooler motivational stories and cool shape shifting scenes? Are you a little rebel angel? The next time it rains will you think that maybe there are angels and maybe they are really crying? Would the world be a better place if we did have at least one fishermen church in every town? A typical town maybe has five Baptist or fifteen Christian churches' so who is right? I see a lot of church's close, why? Maybe finally people are realizing what these preachers are preaching does not make sense. Is Avalon the answer for everyone? No, of Course not. There will always be other churches there will always be a few not wanting to agree or disagree. Is Christianity as we know it in a decline?" The camera zooms in as the movie is about to be over, the camera see's the old man's eyes turn glossy black again showing the demon is back inside again. the old man sits his drink down on the coffee table and reaches up both of his hands toward the camera, smiling, you see His hands again turn into a demonic shapeshifting with long fingernails as he points his fingers at the camera and cups each hand together with the fingers touching, then like a explosion he says boom and his fingers all open wide and you see all ten fingers facing the camera and everything goes black. You realize that is the end, or is it? Does this mean there could be more? The credits roll, black background and white letters showing all the people who made this movie. then a sign that says stay tuned to some of the deleted scenes and behind the camera scenes, so you watch to see what all that is about. Yes, some of the people involved in making this into a movie now get their moment of fame, you see in big letters this movie was based on the book/screenplay Brotherhood by Melvin Abercrombie available at Amazon and other fine bookstores, even he needs his little bit of advertisement and now seeing all the deleted scenes the goof ups and blunders just like any movie. Then you see Rex the cowboy and Jasmine walking along a typical street they see a grocery store that has two kids horse's out front, like the old days, mom would put a dime and the Horse would rock back n forth, rex smiles and says you want to go out in style? jasmine laughs saying "why not" they both climb on the toy horses and rex puts a dime in each one, as the horses jump up and down, the movie camera moves to the old west, they are riding off

in the sunset and you hear the song by Roy
Rodgers and Dale Evans Happy Trails to you,
until we meet again as they ride off in the sunset,
Rex takes His hat off and yells "yippie ya, get
along little doggies" .so is this the end of the
book? can we add more?   "Howdy again, this is
rex rogers and jasmine lee, the two bodyguards
in the movie. Just to give you a thumbs up on
what is happening, Yes, we got married and glad
to say my beautiful wife is expecting" The
camera zooms in on her smiling face and bulging
belly showing she is pregnant." wanted you to
know the old man is working on a new movie and
a new book to follow this one, actually he is re-
writing the Avalon book so you get to see more
scenes, more of us, let me warn you though He is
a stubborn old cuss, and says the same thing
over and over again. guess that was how he was
taught, does get under your skin a little and
aggravates you but deep down we now know
what he is saying is true. We did take two months
off for our Honeymoon I got to go to Japan and
meet her family, pretty interesting some are just
like us stubborn and old fashioned, and the
younger ones accepted me as a cool cowboy. I
learned a lot about Her Buddha and even took
some karate class lessons and now have a new
love for the oriental culture as a whole. The next
book, Avalon Fishermen church is not just a
physical Church. I guess if you got the money,
you could build a physical Avalon Fishermen
church in your town. Get a preacher and staff and
pay so you can go their once or twice a week.
The old fart is 72 and he keeps telling me 60
years ago when he was a kid, he read the book
about King Arthur and the knights of the round
table and their search for the holy grail. We are a
lot younger then that but I too remember reading
about the round table and sir Lancelot and
Guinevere, the secret romance and have seen
many versions on tv I love the Sean Connery
version myself others like the Jax who played on
sons of anarchy, then there are many other
versions most show the old king Arthur wounded

and dying and where do they take him? To the Island of Avalon. So now Avalon is not an actual Island or an actual church, it is a state of mind you can enjoy 24 hours a day, 7 days a week and 365 days a year. It's not just physical but also mental and spiritual, so is the Brotherhood, but then I am getting ahead of myself and spoiling all the fun." He stops and the camera zooms in on Jasmine and now she talks: " I was born and raised in Japan and my family did teach me the way of buddha, in school they thought it would be helpful to learn the English language to get along with them, so we understood their God and their belief system was very scattered and confused to say the least. In Japan and most of the orient you are taught one religion and that is buddha. there are no hundred different Christian belief systems and a wild diversity of other religions its only buddha's oriental government and the Japanese government do speak different languages, yes, Chinese, Korean, Viet Nam, and Japanese even mandarin. Our oriental government has our own way of helping the homeless we have our own system of welfare, food stamps and housing. We look at the stupid laws of the United States and see turmoil by giving anyone, at any time, free welfare, free food stamps, free section 8 housing then do not blame the people for coming over to get free stuff. you want to change the problem? stop the free stuff. I came to America to go to the police academy school. I became a citizen of the United States and have lived here now for the last ten years. The good thing about this Brotherhood is they understand all religions. They realize that we are all here for a different reason to experience different things. Buddha is a male dominant religion where the female is not equal but does teach re-Incarnation according to karma. I have lived many past lifetimes and now convinced rex this makes sense" She stops looks over at Rex and he shakes his head smiling in agreement then she continues " my country, Japan and most of the orient are aware of this new world order and these billionaires trying to make one language, English the only language but we do not ever see that happening. The oriental group under buddha may one day try to get all oriental people to speak one language but again the Chinese wants us to speak their language and our Japanese wants everyone else to speak their language. the scary part is most all of the Orient are learning this English language to get along with the great power of the United States of America. Remember history proves this new world order has been going around for the last two thousand years from the time change from Bc to Ad, so we do not foresee a real difference except the power of these books. If the energy forces out there today are opening up to allow this Avalon to help show the world the olde world order or do the energy forces now want this one male God to rule everything and unite lucifer, buddha, Allah Yahweh, Jehovah and whatever male name you want to call this one male dominant God. I have read many books about wicca trying to bring back the female to this creation process but again there you have a dominant female as Goddess and the male comes by during the phases of spring to be her lover, her consort. buddha has many lovers, many consorts so its ok for a male to have many wives or lovers but let a female do this and she is a whore, a bitch or a prostitute does that sound equal to you?" She pauses for a drink and walks into the kitchen Melvin looks at the camera and says " I have been up there soaring with the eagles and I had to have this wreck to be brought down to nothing. I needed to experience that, I pray and hope you never have to experience that, but that was just me, God gave me another chance and now hopefully this will sink in and make you a better person, that is what these books are about. Seems to me sometimes we need to look at the big picture from a different angle, instead of spending billions of dollars building a wall to keep others out, use that money to help other countries create their own welfare system in their country. Let us take Mexico for example, there is very beautiful ocean front property and beautiful islands, and poverty is rampant, why? we have a few rich drug lords, rich gangs and rich mafia controlling the nation. They just send their bad criminals here to get rid of them and let America handle the problem, America gives them free welfare, free food stamps and free section 8 housing they get rid of their bad people and a few family members, Can we send police and army down there, stop the evil and get the nation where tourist will come down there? The tourist trade is not at all now give the peso a raise, create their own welfare system in every city, every island and create low-cost housing for the needy, this will create many jobs for the trade, then people will not have to come to America, divide families up and take a job they do not want and have to send money back to their families just to survive. Mexico has billions of dollars; all they have to do is print more. That is what we do, need money? just print more, we are so for in debt any way to who? Who do we ever pay this debt to? Obama gave Iran a billion dollars why? how did we as a government allow him to just give a nation a billion dollars? They could have created their own welfare system help their own Islam people and build low cost section8 housing for the needy and build their own country up, instead they spent it on nuclear warfare and more battle ships so they could control the seas. The United States is a Christian nation will always be we allow other religions here as fellow brothers and sisters as long as they do not try to change our belief system. I realize there are good Islam and evil Islam just like there are good Christian's and evil Christian's. spending billions of dollars building a wall will not solve our problem. Helping other countries create their own welfare system taking care of their own people so they will not have to come here will. There will always be rich people, there will always be poor people we all are on a different step. you can come back two years from now and see some on the same step others moved up or down that is what we all need to experience. Why are you here? What do you need to experience during this lifetime? Can you experience everything you want to in only one lifetime? No of course not Can you experience everything you want to in a hundred lifetimes? We have the resources and the money to help other countries, these are our brother and sisters. God is looking down on what you are doing, you came into this world with nothing, and you will leave this world with nothing who you are, what you done who you helped, you all will be judged, I hope my books touched you, I hope my books helped you move up another step. I hope you will reach out and help someone else move up another step. That is what life is all about, make the world a better place, enjoy life, God created a beautiful world go see it, enjoy it, touch others, Thank you " The old man hands the micro phone to rex "Ok that was fun we do not want to spoil everything the camera crew has the option of going back and showing some of the deleted scenes and the ones we made mistakes on so the world knows all this is just acting. no one was actually shot or killed just catsup or movie blood and some great special effect scenes and now you get to see Lucifer flying around with all the cables and wires and the crane holding him up and the crew how they made some of these special effect scenes. they need there five minutes of fame, get to tell their name, a little about them and what they do and how they accomplish these special effects. some ideas are still trade secrets so they do not want you to see everything The Hidden Camera knows they are about to roll the credits, who was all in the movie, the hidden camera goes back to the mansion, the old man is setting in his recliner enjoying a tall margarita with a umbrella in his drink, he looks up, sets down the drink on the coffee table, smiling you see his eyes turn a glossy black for one more time, He holds his hands up to show you his fingerprints and they shape shift into this demonic hands again, as he opens his hands a little you see his face behind the hands and he curls them up into a ball and says a very loud

Boom smiling his curled up hands spread out real fast to show the loud boom and everything goes black. You see the black background with white letters showing all the different people it took to make the movie. I keep having this same dream over and over, I am walking somewhere, and I am lost, trying to find my way home. I realize all my books and most of the other books out there do not have a happy ending so what is the happy ending? Do I ever find my way home? Do I finally get to set in my mansion in heaven forever and ever? Will I be lost up there with millions of mansions or ivory towers, can I be happy with a small cottage? What will I do in a mansion anyway? I am still looking for home, I finally realize I am at home, I found the last secret key to happiness, Let go and let God, the Blessed Assurance that where ever I am, whatever rode I am traveling on, all I got to do is raise my hands up and thank God, Thank the Goddess, thank you Jesus Christ the Ha mashiach , looks like I will be moving to California to make these books/screenplays into a movie series thank you for reading

End of Psychosomatic, all acts, all scenes.